Whitestein Series in Software Agent Technologies and Autonomic Computing

Series Editors:
Marius Walliser
Stefan Brantschen
Monique Calisti
Marc Herbstritt

This series reports new developments in agent-based software technologies and agent-oriented software engineering methodologies, with particular emphasis on applications in the area of autonomic computing & communications.

The spectrum of the series includes research monographs, high quality notes resulting from research and industrial projects, outstanding Ph.D. theses, and the proceedings of carefully selected conferences. The series is targeted at promoting advanced research and facilitating know-how transfer to industrial use.

About Whitestein Technologies

Whitestein Technologies is a leading innovator in the area of software agent technologies and autonomic computing & communications. Whitestein Technologies' offering includes advanced products, solutions, and services for various applications and industries, as well as a comprehensive middleware for the development and operation of autonomous, self-managing, and self-organizing systems and networks.
Whitestein Technologies' customers and partners include innovative global enterprises, service providers, and system integrators, as well as universities, technology labs, and other research institutions.

www.whitestein.com

Huiye Ma
Ho-fung Leung

Bidding Strategies in Agent-Based Continuous Double Auctions

Birkhäuser
Basel · Boston · Berlin

Authors:

Huiye Ma
Centrum voor Wiskunde en Informatica (CWI)
Kruislaan 413
1098 SJ Amsterdam
Netherlands
e-mail: ma@cwi.nl

Ho-fung Leung
Department of Computer Science and
Engineering
The Chinese University of Hong Kong
Shatin, New Territories
Hong Kong, PR China
e-mail: lhf@cuhk.edu.hk

2000 Mathematical Subject Classification: 68-02, 68T05, 68T37, 68W01

Library of Congress Control Number: 2008927822

Bibliographic information published by Die Deutsche Bibliothek
Die Deutsche Bibliothek lists this publication in the Deutsche Nationalbibliografie;
detailed bibliographic data is available in the Internet at <http://dnb.ddb.de>.

ISBN 978-3-7643-8729-7 Birkhäuser Verlag AG, Basel – Boston – Berlin

© 2008 Birkhäuser Verlag, P.O. Box 133, CH-4010 Basel, Switzerland
Part of Springer Science+Business Media
Printed on acid-free paper produced from chlorine-free pulp. TCF ∞

ISBN 978-3-7643-8729-7   ISBN 978-3-7643-8730-3 (eBook)
DOI 10.1007/978-3-7643-8730-3
9 8 7 6 5 4 3 2 1

www.birkhauser.ch

Contents

Preface

Continuous Double Auction (CDA) is an efficient market institution for real-world trading. Negotiation capabilities for software agents are a central concern. Especially, agents need to be able to prepare bids for and evaluate offers on behalf of the users they represent, with the aim of obtaining the maximum benefit for their users. They do this according to some bidding strategies. However, in many cases, on the one hand, determining which strategy to employ is a complex decision-making task because of the inherent uncertainty and dynamics of the auction market; on the other hand, strategies described in the literature do not adapt very well to dynamic markets. To this end, this book is concerned with developing novel bidding strategies for CDAs and enhancing the performance of different strategies in CDAs with respect to adaptivity by designing some tools for general use.

In this book, we focus on two types of CDAs. One is the CDA with a deadline of an inactive interval. Another is the CDA with a fixed deadline. Three kinds of adaptive behaviours are proposed to enhance the performance of the most widely adopted strategies in CDAs in the literature. They are adaptive softness, adaptive judgement of price acceptability, and adaptive time strategies. First, in the CDA with a deadline of an inactive interval, we design novel adaptive strategies, named Adaptive Attitude strategies, based on eagerness. Eagerness indicates the current supply and demand relationship from the agent's own point of view. To compute the value of eagerness, fuzzy sets and fuzzy logic are used to cope with the significant degrees of uncertainty in CDA markets. We define two kinds of adaptive behaviours: adaptive softness and adaptive judgement of price acceptability. Both of them resemble human traders' behaviours to compromise and set thresholds on acceptable prices in the trading process of real-life markets and can enhance the performance of various strategies. Secondly, in CDAs with a fixed deadline, we ourselves research the time strategies. In this market, every agent is aware of importance of timing. Therefore adaptive time strategies are introduced to guide the agent to arrange his behaviour according to time, which can enhance the performance of different strategies. Both the novel strategies and the enhanced strategies have been demonstrated to be superior in a wide range of CDA circumstances. We show that eagerness is a practical solution for this class of application. We believe that this work represents an important step towards adapting agents in auctions.

Through the work described in this book, Adaptive Attitude (AA) strategies have been demonstrated to be superior in a wide range of CDA scenarios. Moreover, three kinds of adaptive behaviours have been shown to greatly enhance the performance of the most widely adopted strategies in CDAs.

Chapter 1

Introduction

1.1 Agent-Based Auctions in Electronic Commerce

1.1.1 Auctions in Electronic Commerce

With the advent of global computer networks, in particular the Internet and the World Wide Web, electronic commerce (e-commerce) has been taking an increasingly important role in many organizations [50]. It provides a faster, cheaper, more personalized, and more agile way for businesses to interact with their customers and their suppliers. Auctions of various kinds are efficient mechanisms to allocate resources in electronic commerce. In this context, online auctions, institutions where goods are traded on the Internet by the process of bidding and allocating through competition, are among the most widely studied and employed means of interaction [5]. Such online auctions are prevalent because they are an efficient and effective method of allocating goods or services [128], [103], [93].

Auctions come in many different forms, each with its own rules and ensuing properties [99], [97], [114]. In *English auctions* [20], [65], the auctioneer starts with a reservation price and solicits successively higher public bids from the bidders until no one increases the bid, and the last bidder is the winner. *First-price sealed bid* (*FPSB*) and *second-price sealed bid* (*SPSB*, also called *Vickrey*) auctions are auctions in which bidders submit sealed bids to the auctioneer and the bidder who submits the highest bid wins [65]. In FPSB, the winner pays the highest bid. In SPSB, the bidder wins but pays the second highest bid [114]. In *Dutch auctions*, the auctioneer starts with a high price and decreases it until a bidder accepts the current price. In *continuous double auctions* (*CDA*), buyers submit increasingly higher bids and sellers submit increasingly lower asks at any moment during a trading period and transactions occurs when the highest bid is at least as high as the lowest ask [41], [29], [20], [36], [96].

On the basis of the classical auction types described above, variants have been designed in recent years. For examples, a *combinatorial auction* [56], [57],

[47], [118], [55], [129], [23] is a type of auction where bidders can submit bids to buy a bundle of multiple goods. In sequential or simultaneous *multiple auctions*, a bidder needs to monitor all the relevant auctions, decide which one to bid in, and determine what to bid in order to get the goods at the best deal [91], [9], [110], [32], [51], [38], [39], [40], [33], [132]. In *multi-attribute auctions*, multiple attributes of the goods, such as delivery date, efficiency, volume, *etc.*, are considered by bidders, who aim at obtaining an overall rating for the bid from ratings of the individual attributes of the bid [26], [44], [66]. Besides these variants of auctions, most recently, online search engine advertising has become an appealing approach to highly targeted advertising, and is the major source of revenue for modern web search engines such as Google[1] and Yahoo![2] [11]. The process of determining which ads get assigned to which keywords and how much each advertiser pays is resolved via keyword auctions. Advertisers choose which keywords they want to bid on and participate in Generalized Second-Price auctions for those keywords [30].

Auction scenarios consist of two clearly distinct components: *protocols* and *strategies* [7]. The former defines the valid behaviours of agents during interactions. For example, in an English auction, an agent needs to bid at the current price plus a bid increment. The latter is the method an agent employs to achieve his negotiation objectives within the specified protocol. For example, in an English auction, a strategy that could be adopted is to bid a small amount more than the current highest bid and to stop bidding when the agent's reservation price is reached. Generally speaking, the protocol is set by the marketplace owner before execution, and is publicly known to all the participants. In contrast, the strategy is determined by each individual participant and is typically private. Nevertheless, protocols and strategies are inextricably linked because the effectiveness of a strategy is very much determined by the protocol. Thus a strategy that is effective for one protocol may perform very poorly or may even be invalid for other protocols. Moreover, for some protocols, the optimal bidding strategy is easy to determine and simple to compute. For example, the strategy proposed above for an English auction is in fact optimal if all the agents have their private valuations of the goods. However, generally there is no such simple solution and developing a good strategy is a significant research challenge.

1.1.2   Agent-Based Auctions in Electronic Commerce

In order to harness the full potential of various types of auctions, it is important to increase both the degree and the sophistication of the automation. To achieve this, *software agents* are needed, which are representatives of human users to fulfil their requirements and expectations and consequently need to be tailored to achieve those humans' aims [95]. A key aspect of such trading agents is that they need to interact with one another in order to affect trades (*i.e.*, to buy and sell goods or services) [58].

---

[1] http://adwords.google.com/.
[2] http://www.yahoo.com/.

In such environments, agents can perform a variety of different roles: (i) monitoring auctions in order to keep the user informed of the latest progress of various auctions, (ii) analyzing the market situation and history in order to predict probable trends, (iii) deciding when, how many and how much to bid in order to get the best deals.

The more these activities can be automated, the more time can be saved for the user. Moreover, in complex settings agents are likely to be more effective than human bidders. This is partly a matter of speed (agents can process information more quickly than humans), but also because agents can more easily and more systematically perform the complex decision making required to operate effectively in multiple auction settings. Preliminary evidence for this [25] shows that software agents outperform their human counterparts in continuous double auctions. Using software agents can thus increase the chance of obtaining the goods and bringing greater profit and satisfaction for the user [2], [26], [32], [91], [107]. When more agents are used in the market, the market becomes more efficient [91]. Based on these factors, automation of bidding becomes possible, in which agents carry out trading, and hence human traders can save considerable time and effort [6].

1.1.3 Motivations of this Work

Automation of bidding is complex. Given the variety of auction protocols, it is perhaps not surprising that the bidding strategies of the participants cover a similarly broad spectrum of behaviours. In short, there is no optimal strategy that can be used in all cases. To be effective, bidding strategies need to be tailored to the type of the auction in which they are to be used. Perhaps the key challenge in this area is to design effective and efficient strategies that agents can use to guide their bidding behaviour. Although challenging, such developments are necessary if trading agents are to realise their full potential. Furthermore, we believe that the existence of effective strategies will mean that online auctions can be more readily deployed as a practical market protocol. Given this background, the research reported in this book addresses exactly this challenge for a complex and dynamic e-commerce auction scenario, continuous double auctions.

If we take a look at human traders in real-life markets, the following situations can be detected. When human traders buy or sell goods in the CDA market, they will naturally develop some subjective feelings. In particular, when it is difficult to trade goods, human traders will be eager for more transactions, on the totality of which they hope to gain more profit. On the other hand, if they find it easy to trade goods, they will be tempted to obtain more profit in each transaction so as to earn more profit in the end. Eagerness is a natural feeling for human traders. Besides the feeling of eagerness, human traders may make different degrees of compromise in return for more transactions when encountering some difficulties in trading; they may set thresholds on the price acceptable to them in the current market and adjust the values of the thresholds with the dynamic market, both of which will improve profit. The feeling of eagerness of human traders also inspires agents to develop eagerness with the market on the basis of the trading history of the market, which tells the agent whether it is easy or difficult to trade. Guided by eagerness, an agent is able to behave adaptively to make compromises or to judge the price acceptability with the dynamic market. However, little work has been done in bidding negotiation to simulate human traders' feeling and behaviours in real-life markets. With the aim of more adaptive and efficient strategies, we develop new tools for general use to enable agents utilizing existing bidding strategies to behave more adaptively to enhance their profit.

Another case that we notice in real-life markets is that many online auctions have a fixed deadline before which the trading process must be terminated. Therefore human traders in the auctions take a time effect into account when bidding. When it is easy for human traders to make transactions, they will wait some time before really getting involved in the trading process. Otherwise, they will speed up their bidding process if possible before each bid submission. This kind of behaviour will usually benefit human traders. Given this, time strategies are proposed in agent-based continuous double auctions with a fixed deadline where each round is terminated within a pre-specified deadline. Agents in this kind of continuous double auctions are aware of the time, including the current time and the deadlines. Nevertheless, the effect of time strategies in such types of continuous double auctions has never been investigated. Hence, we seek to develop adaptive time strategies to enhance existing strategies for this case.

1.2   Research Aims

In designing new bidding strategies to enhance existing bidding strategies for CDAs, there are a number of common issues that need to be dealt with. In addition, we believe that it is possible to identify a range of concepts and technologies that form a solid foundation for tackling such problems in a broad range of situations. We now consider each of these in turn.

First, an agent needs to be adaptive so that he can tailor his bidding strategy according to latest state of the environment in which he is situated. Being adaptive is particularly important in cases where the environment is subject to changes. These can happen, for example, when the agent is trading with the same (or similar) partners or opponents repeatedly. In such cases, the agent can adapt his behaviours according to the behaviour of other agents so that he can obtain a better payoff. However, when things changed, often due to the introduction of new traders, the parameters which characterise the strategy need to be changed accordingly. This is impractical to achieve by manually adjusting the parameters, since this is a complex and error-prone process. So it is desirable that the agent adapt himself autonomously.

Second, an agent needs to make some degree of compromise when generating and responding to bids. For example, in a CDA, if a buyer agent is going to bid $100, but the lowest ask in the market is $101, then the buyer agent may benefit by compromising and bidding 1% higher than he is going to bid in order to make the trade.

Third, an agent needs to be flexible in setting and adjusting thresholds of acceptable price according to the latest state of his environment. This procedure is usually based on the agent's ability to detect the market environment in real time so that the values of thresholds can be adjusted in a meaningful way. In details, if a seller has many transactions recently, he should set the thresholds high; if a seller seldom makes transactions, should will set the thresholds low. When using the same strategy, adjusting thresholds of acceptable price adaptively can make a significant difference to the outcomes obtained.

Fourth, an agent needs to be able to manage his behaviours by time if there is a fixed deadline to terminate each round of a CDA. With a fixed deadline, if a human trader finds that he can easily trade all his goods, then he should not be anxious and should be willing to wait for some time before beginning to trade in each round.

Given these aims, we propose to use a range of techniques based on fuzzy set theory to cope with the inherent uncertainty present in all of these activities. This uncertainty can come from a number of sources including sellers, buyers, the supply and demand relationship in the market, or the remaining time before the deadline. For example, the number of traders and the decision strategy of the other traders are generally unknown to an agent. Fuzzy set theory has proved to be effective to handle uncertainties in a range of applications [34], [131], [53]. Moreover, the intuitive nature of fuzzy logic and its embodiment in fuzzy rules make it readily comprehensible to agent designers.

This work is concerned with the design of bidding strategies for continuous double auctions and techniques enhancing different bidding strategies for continuous double auctions. The first aspect of our work involves developing novel strategies for buyer agents and seller agents in CDAs. Specifically, a buyer agent needs to decide when to place a bid and at what price; a seller agent needs to decide when to place an ask and at what price. The other major purpose of this work is to explore the design and implementation of general tools to enhance the performance of various strategies in CDAs that exist in the literature. To effect such performance enhancement, an agent needs to: (i) adapt himself to suit the prevailing market context, such as the change in the demand and supply in the market and other bidders' strategies; (ii) make compromises with his bids and asks so that he can get more transactions when encountering difficulties in trading; (iii) set price thresholds on the acceptable asks or bids; (iv) make good use of time when trading in continuous double auctions with a fixed deadline.

1.3 Research Contributions

The work described in this book makes a number of contributions to the state of the art in the area of bidding strategies that autonomous trading agents can use in a number of CDAs. Specifically,

- We develop a novel Adaptive Attitude (AA) bidding strategy that agents can use to participate in CDAs [67] [73]. The effectiveness of the strategy is demonstrated by empirically benchmarking it against the major strategies that have been proposed in the literature. The evaluation shows that our AA strategy is superior in a wide range of market situations.

- We propose to use soft asks and soft bids in agent-based CDAs [68]. An agent changes his ask or bid to a soft ask or soft bid by adding a degree of softness around the determined value. An adaptive mechanism is developed for agents to vary the degree according to their perception of the marketplace in which they are operating. This mechanism has been tested on the major strategies for CDAs and empirically demonstrates its ability to remarkably enhance their performance.

- We define and implement, for the first time, an adaptive judgement of price acceptability that an agent can use to set thresholds for the asks or bids [70]. If the outstanding ask or the outstanding bid is very profitable, then the agent can directly accept it. If the outstanding ask or the bid is very poor, then the agent can decline it right away. Experimental results show that, after integrating the adaptive judgement of price acceptability, an agent attains a higher overall performance.

- We introduce for the first time adaptive time strategies for agents to utilize in continuous double auctions with a fixed deadline [71]. If it is easy to trade his goods, an agent should wait for some time before beginning the process. Otherwise, the agent should try to expedite his bidding process. A special market situation, illusory seller's or buyer's market, is defined. An illusory seller's market (buyer's market) occurs when supply is larger (smaller) than demand whilst the seller (buyer) finds it is easy to trade his goods. To cope with an illusory seller's or buyer's market, circumstance-dependent negative softness is proposed, which enables agents to increase profit without making compromises. Experimental results show that an agent experienced with integrating adaptive time strategies in a wide range of continuous double auctions with a fixed deadline attains a better performance than a corresponding agent without such experience.

1.4 Book Structure

The rest of this book is structured in the following manner:

Chapter 2 surveys agent-based continuous double auctions and bidding strategies. For the former, we define agents in CDA scenarios and then give the basic continuous double auction mechanism and its variants. For the latter, strategies of agents in CDAs as reported in the literature are introduced and discussed. Evaluation criteria of the strategies and methodologies to analyze them are presented and investigated as well.

Chapter 3 concentrates on CDAs and new algorithms are designed for buyer and seller agents. Eagerness is first defined based on short-term attitude and long-term attitude in order to reflect the current supply and demand relationship from the agent's own point of view. Moreover, we show how an agent can, with the guidance of eagerness, dynamically adjust his bidding behaviour to respond effectively to changes in the marketplace . We then demonstrate, by empirical evaluations, how our agents outperform other agents, employing six conventional strategies previously developed for CDAs in the literature.

Chapter 4 defines soft asks and soft bids, and an adaptive mechanism is designed that a software agent can use to adaptively adjust the degree of softness with the dynamic CDA market. The notion of eagerness is extended from that in Chapter 3. Fuzzy sets and fuzzy logic are employed to determine the value of eagerness. The effectiveness of the adaptive mechanism is empirically illustrated, i.e., when an agent (using any of five major bidding strategies previously developed for CDAs) incorporates the adaptive mechanism, his performance is generally enhanced a lot in a wide range of CDA market scenarios.

Chapter 5 gives the definitions of the judgement of price acceptability for seller agents and buyer agents. An adaptive mechanism is proposed and implemented. A software agent can use the mechanism to adaptively adjust the thresholds of price acceptability according to eagerness. Empirical evaluation demonstrates that agents, employing the major bidding strategies for CDAs proposed in the literature, can remarkably enhance their performance in general in a wide range of market scenarios after integrating the adaptive mechanism.

Chapter 6 discusses strategies used in continuous double auctions with a fixed deadline where each round of CDAs is ended within a fixed deadline. In such CDA markets, agents are aware of both the current time and the deadline. Time strategies are established and adaptive mechanisms are designed for the first time. In particular, an illusory seller's or buyer's market is identified. Circumstance-dependent negative softness is proposed to handle this special market situation. We show, through empirical evaluation against a number of bidding strategies proposed for CDAs in the literature, that agents employing the adaptive mechanism perform effectively and robustly in a wide range of CDA scenarios.

Chapter 7 discusses the main characteristics of the CDA markets we focus on in this book. A comparison between the agent-based CDA markets discussed in this book and the CDA markets in real life is given. We then discuss the conditions under which strategies and tools proposed in this book are applicable.

Chapter 8 concludes the book. We recap the main contributions of this book and describe pathways for future work.

Chapter 2

Agent-Based CDAs and Bidding Strategies

2.1 Agent-Based Continuous Double Auctions

The role of agents in auctions is to represent their users, who may be buyers or sellers or the auctioneer, to achieve particular objectives [58], [54], [81], [83], [50]. Although there are many attributes concluded in the literature, some attributes are essential for CDAs we discuss in this book. First of all, we define exactly what we mean by the term "agent" in CDAs. An *agent in CDAs* is a software package that can be viewed as a delegate of his[1] user to achieve a good performance which usually means a good profit. To this end, an agent must exhibit the following properties:

- Autonomy: The agent is capable of making decisions about what actions to take without constantly referring back to his user;

- Adaptivity: The agent is capable of adjusting himself to environmental conditions based on trading history, *etc.*;

Except for these two properties as a must, an agent may possess one or more of the following attributes conditioned on the specific environment where he is situated [50], [81], [127]:

- Proactiveness: The agent is capable of taking the initiative rather than acting simply in response to his environment;

- Reactivity: The agent is capable of responding appropriately to the prevailing circumstances in dynamic environments;

---

[1]The reader will note that we now refer to the agent with words such as "his" rather than "its" in order to emphasize the human-like functioning of the agent.

- Prediction: The agent is capable of anticipating future trading trends and guiding his behaviour towards it.

- Social ability: The agent is capable of interacting with other agents and possibly with humans via some communication language;

- Ability to learn: The agent is capable of learning to understand the user's preferences and behaviour, to cope with new situations he may face and to improve his performance over time;

- Mobility: The agent is capable of travelling through a network.

When we put such agents into CDA markets, we consider the following scenarios as examples of what will be possible in agent-based continuous double auctions.

Scenario 1: From the perspective of a buyer. A buyer decides that he would like to buy the book "Sense and Sensibility" in an online auction market. He can see the current highest bid is \$19.5 and the lowest ask is \$33. He thinks that he will not buy this book if the current bid is above \$27 or the auction cannot stop before Jane's birthday, Feb. 28, because he wants to buy this book as a birthday gift for her. It is rational that the buyer wants to save some money if possible. Finally he computes a bid according to the days left and the competition level in the auction combined with his eagerness to get this book. Therefore, when a buyer agent determines his bid to be submitted, he needs to consider the time, the supply and demand relationship, and his feeling.

Scenario 2: From the perspective of a seller. A seller wishes to sell his old piano in an auction market for second-hand goods. According to his experience on the price for such a piano, he sets his anticipated transaction price to be above \$2000. After a period of trading, to his surprise, many buyers come and bid for this piano and there is little competition from other sellers. The current highest bid is \$2300. Encouraged by the increasing trend of bids, the seller decides to increase his anticipated transaction price to be above \$2500. At last, the seller trades his piano successfully at the price \$2550. The above scenario shows that a seller agent takes into account the current supply and demand relationship and the trading experience and adjusts his threshold on price with the changing market.

Both of the above scenarios demonstrate that an agent in CDAs needs to be autonomous since humans will usually leave their agents in the market without constantly checking status. The agent will form his understanding of the market based on his trading experience. His individual understanding will cause him to have some feelings toward the market, *e.g.*, eagerness; and his feeling will fluctuate with the market from time to time. This kind of feeling enables the agent to adjust his behaviours with the dynamic market. As a consequence the agent is adaptive because he will take actions considering the current market situation and his own feeling toward the market, *etc.*

2.2 Continuous Double Auction Mechanisms

2.2.1 Basic CDA Mechanisms

A CDA [36] is a marketplace where there are agents selling goods (*sellers*) and agents buying goods (*buyers*). The sellers and buyers in one CDA market trade single-type (homogeneous) goods. An *ask* is the price submitted by a seller to sell a unit of goods. Similarly, a *bid* is the amount submitted by a buyer to buy a unit of goods. Sellers and buyers can submit their asks and bids at any time during a CDA. The current lowest ask in the market is called the *outstanding ask*, denoted as oa. The current highest bid in the market is called the *outstanding bid*, denoted as ob. A *valid ask* is an ask lower than the current oa. Hence oa is decreased by sellers' valid asks during a round. Any ask not lower than oa is called an *invalid ask* and ignored by the market. A *valid bid* is a bid higher than the current ob. Therefore ob is increased by buyers' bids during a round. Any bid not higher than ob is called an *invalid bid* and ignored by the market.

For each seller or buyer, there is an *acceptable price range* $[P_{ll}, P_{ul}]$ for a CDA market. P_{ll} is the lowest acceptable price in the market and P_{ul} is the highest acceptable price in the market, which are formed on the basis of the seller or buyer's experience and the trading history of the market. For a seller or buyer agent, each unit of goods has a *reservation price*. If a seller submits an ask lower than the reservation price, he will lose profit. If a buyer submits a bid higher than the reservation price, he will also lose profit.

When ob is higher than or equal to oa, the seller who submits oa and the buyer who submits ob make a *transaction*. The *transaction price* is equal to the earlier one of ob and oa. When there is a transaction or there is no new ob or oa in a pre-specified time, a *round* is terminated. After the current round terminates, a new round can begin. In each round, at most one unit of goods is transacted. When all the sellers have sold all the units of goods or all the buyers have bought all the units of goods, a *run* is terminated. A run is often composed of multiple rounds. The *supply* of a CDA is defined to be the total number of units of goods that all the sellers need to sell in a run. The *demand* is defined to be the total number of units of goods that all the buyers desire to buy in a run. For example, the supply of a CDA market is 30 and the demand is 40. Thus there are 30 rounds in a run of the CDA market. The pseudo code of the *basic CDA mechanism* is shown in Figure 2.1.

2.2.2 Variants of Basic CDA Mechanisms

Some variants of CDAs have been proposed by many researchers. Preist *et al.* [90] describes a new agent-based market mechanism for online commodity trading, called iterated double auction, where agents first enter the mock marketplace to determine the equilibrium price; after the equilibrium price is found, all trades actually take place at this price.

1: P_{ul} and P_{ll} are formed on the market trading history;
2: $r = 0$;
3: **while** $r \leq min(supply, demand)$ **do**
4: 　$oa = P_{ul}$; $ob = P_{ll}$;
5: 　**while** true **do**
6: 　　**nondetermistic** choice
7: 　　　**case** a buyer submits a bid:
8: 　　　　**if** $bid \leq ob$ or out of $[P_{ll}, P_{ul}]$ **then**
9: 　　　　　bid is an invalid bid;
10: 　　　　**else**
11: 　　　　　bid updates ob and becomes a new ob;
12: 　　　　**end if**
13: 　　　　**if** $ob \geq oa$ **then**
14: 　　　　　$P_t = oa$; The round is ended;
15: 　　　　**end if**
16: 　　　**case** a seller submits an ask:
17: 　　　　**if** $ask \geq oa$ or out of $[P_{ll}, P_{ul}]$ **then**
18: 　　　　　ask is an invalid ask;
19: 　　　　**else**
20: 　　　　　ask updates oa and becomes a new oa;
21: 　　　　**end if**
22: 　　　　**if** $ob \geq oa$ **then**
23: 　　　　　$P_t = ob$; The round is ended;
24: 　　　　**end if**
25: 　　　**case** time out:
26: 　　　　**if** no new oa or ob in a pre-specified time period **then**
27: 　　　　　The round is ended with no transaction;
28: 　　　　**end if**
29: 　　**end nondetermistic** choice;
30: 　**end while**
31: 　$r = r + 1$;
32: **end while**

Figure 2.1: The pseudo code of the basic CDA mechanism.

Another form of continuous double auction is persistent shout double auction [102] which is a well established mechanism used in the international financial markets. In this market, a trader may make a bid or ask at any time, but once made it persists until the trader chooses to alter it or remove it, or it is accepted. Preist and Tol [92] consider the persistent shout double auction as a more realistic form of double auction market.

Ma and Leung [71] have done research into time strategies in continuous double auction where each round is terminated by a pre-specified fixed deadline, called *CDAs with a fixed deadline*. This CDA mechanism is different from the CDA in Section 2.2.1 in the following aspects. The maximum time length to terminate each round is specified in advance and is called a fixed deadline. At any time within the fixed deadline, a seller is free to accept the highest bid and a buyer is free to accept the lowest ask of sellers. If there is a transaction, or the pre-specified fixed deadline is reached, a round is terminated.

Accompanied by the increasing use of the Internet and agents, online auctions are widely accepted and changing traditional viewpoints on auctions. As a result, some issues are shown to be more and more important especially for online auction markets, such as security [120], [112], [60], [121], [35], [104], [46], [82], [122], [13], and trust [37], [75], [111], [80], [61], [8], [12], [98], [125], [126], *etc.* We know that security and trust issues also exist in continuous double auctions. However, security and trust are not our focus in this book. Therefore, we assume that there is no security or trust problems for our work in this book.

2.3 Bidding Strategies for Agents in CDAs

In this section, we present a framework for designing strategies adopted by trading agents in continuous double auctions, shown in Figure 2.2. This framework is specific in that only bidding strategies of CDAs can be included into it. For a more general framework targeting on various types of auctions, please refer to [117]. Here, our framework is based upon three main observations:

- An agent collects information from his environment and requires information about himself.

- An agent rarely has full information about other agents and the market.

- An agent needs to employ more or less heuristics in his strategy to handle incomplete information and the dynamic market environment.

The framework shown in Figure 2.2 gives the common structure of the strategies adopted by software agents in CDAs. The input for the strategy is information, such as public information and private information. The output for the strategy is the ask or bid to be submitted. Based on the framework, several bidding strategies are described in detail by emphasizing their specific structure with pseudo code.

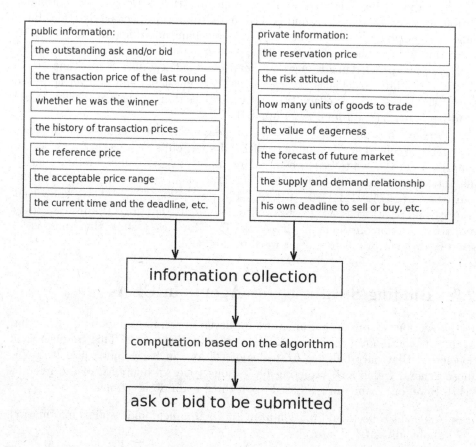

Figure 2.2: The framework for designing various strategies to compute asks or bids in CDAs.

2.3.1 Zero Intelligence Bidding Strategy

Gode and Sunder [42] were the first to design *Zero Intelligence (ZI)* agents. Each ZI agent generates random asks or bids depending on whether he is a seller or a buyer. These asks or bids are distributed independently and uniformly over the entire range of trading prices. The agent does not seek to maximize his profit, and does not observe, remember, or learn. There are two versions of ZI agents, *ZI with Constraint* (ZI-C) agents and *ZI Unconstrained* (ZI-U) agents.

A *ZI-C* agent is a ZI agent who is subject to the budget constraint which forbids the agent to buy or sell at a loss. Thus a ZI-C seller submits an ask which is a random value, less than the highest acceptable price of the market and more than the reservation price of this unit by Equation 2.1.

$$ask = rand(x, P_{ul}),\qquad(2.1)$$

where x is the reservation price of the unit and P_{ul} is the highest acceptable price of the market.

Similarly, a ZI-C buyer submits a bid which is a random value, more than the lowest acceptable price of the market and less than the reservation price of this unit of goods. The computation is shown in Equation 2.2. ZI-C agents are widely adopted as benchmark agents because of their simplicity during implementation.

$$bid = rand(P_{ll}, x),\qquad(2.2)$$

where x is the reservation price of the unit and P_{ll} is the lowest acceptable price of the market.

For a *ZI-U* agent, he is freed from the budget constraint. A ZI-U seller or buyer can submit an ask or a bid which is a random value computed by Equation 2.3, less than the highest acceptable price of the market and more than the lowest acceptable price of the market without regard to the agent's reservation prices. Buyers and sellers are free to engage in money-losing transactions.

$$ask/bid = rand(P_{ll}, P_{ul}).\qquad(2.3)$$

2.3.2 ZIP Bidding Strategy

The *zero-intelligence-plus* (ZIP) strategy was developed by Cliff and Bruten [22], [17], [21]. Each *ZIP* agent has a *profit margin* which determines the difference between the agent's reservation price and the ask or bid to be submitted. If there was a transaction in the last round and the agent was the winner, the agent would increase his profit margin in the current round. If there was a transaction in the last round and the agent was not the winner, or there was no transaction, the agent would decrease his profit margin in the current round. This procedure helps the agent adapt to the dynamic market from time to time and benefits the agent in the end. The central idea of how to adjust the profit margin is shown in Figures 2.3 and 2.4 for sellers and buyers.

```
1: if the last shout was accepted at price q then
2:    any seller for which p_i ≤ q should raise his profit margin;
3:    if the last shout was a bid then
4:       any active seller for which p_i ≥ q should lower his margin;
5:    end if
6: else
7:    if the last shout was an ask then
8:       any active seller for which p_i ≥ q should lower his margin;
9:    end if
10: end if
```

Figure 2.3: The pseudo code of the algorithm for the ZIP sellers.

```
1: if the last shout was accepted at price q then
2:    any buyer for which p_i ≥ q should raise his profit margin;
3:    if the last shout was an ask then
4:       any active buyer for which p_i ≤ q should lower his margin;
5:    end if
6: else
7:    if the last shout was a bid then
8:       any active buyer for which p_i ≤ q should lower his margin;
9:    end if
10: end if
```

Figure 2.4: The pseudo code of the algorithm for the ZIP buyers.

The adaptation mechanism to specify how the profit margins of the sellers and buyers are raised or lowered is given below. At a given time t, an individual ZIP seller or buyer calculates the shout price $p_i(t)$ for a unit j with the reservation price $\lambda_{i,j}$ using the profit margin $\mu_i(t)$ according to the following equation:

$$p_i(t) = \lambda_{i,j}(1 + \mu_i(t)).$$

It is necessary to give an update rule for the profit margin μ_i on the transition from time t to $t+1$ so that $p_i(t)$ is updated from time t to $t+1$ accordingly:

$$\mu_i(t+1) = (p_i(t) + \Delta_i(t)) \div \lambda_{i,j} - 1.$$

Using $\Gamma_i(t)$ in place of $\Delta_i(t)$ gives the following update rule:

$$\mu_i(t+1) = (p_i(t) + \Gamma_i(t)) \div \lambda_{i,j} - 1,$$

where $\Gamma_i(t+1) = \gamma_i \Gamma_i(t) + (1-\gamma_i)\Delta_i(t)$, $\Delta_i(t) = \beta_i(\tau_i(t) - p_i(t))$, $\tau_i(t) = R_i(t)q(t) + A_i(t)$, and $R_i(t)$ and $A_i(t)$ are random reals and $q(t)$ is the last shout. When the intention is to increase the agent's shout price $R_i(t) > 1.0$ and $A_i(t) > 0.0$; when the intention is to decrease it, $0.0 < R_i(t) < 1.0$ and $A_i(t) < 0.0$. Every time the profit margin is altered, the traget price is calculated using the newly generated random values of $R_i(t)$ and $A_i(t)$.

2.3.3 CP Bidding Strategy

Preist and Tol [92] presented a strategy which is based on ZIP strategy. We call it *CP* strategy in this book. The heuristics is simpler than that of ZIP. The main idea of CP strategy is straightforward. If there is no transaction in the current round, an agent should try to be competitive by means of submitting a value slightly better than his rivals. If, on the other hand, there was a transaction in the last round, an agent should submit a value at which he may obtain a trade in the current round. The value is set to be slightly better than the outstanding ask or bid in the last round. This procedure allows the agent to squeeze a little more profit from the market. The pseudo code of the algorithm is shown in Figures 2.5 and 2.6.

By running the algorithms in Figures 2.5 and 2.6, target value can be determined. Given the target value, the agent does not jump straight to that value, but moves towards it at a rate determined by the learning rule. The learning rule used is Widrow-Hoff with momentum. With $p(t)$ and $\tau(t)$, the valuation and target price at time t, the learning rule determines the new valuation, $p(t+1)$, as follows:

$$p(t+1) = \gamma p(t) + (1-\gamma)\beta(\tau(t) - p(t)),$$

where $p(t+1)$ is the ask or the bid to be submitted to the market.

```
1: if oa > ob then
2:     ℘ = r₁ × oa + r₂;
3:     target = oa − ℘;
4: end if
5: if oa ≤ ob then
6:     ℘ = r₁ × ob + r₂;
7:     target = ob + ℘;
8: end if
```

Figure 2.5: The pseudo code of the algorithm for the CP sellers.

```
1: if oa > ob then
2:     ℘ = r₁ × ob + r₂;
3:     target = ob + ℘;
4: end if
5: if oa ≤ ob then
6:     ℘ = r₁ × oa + r₂;
7:     target = oa − ℘;
8: end if
```

Figure 2.6: The pseudo code of the algorithm for the CP buyers.

2.3.4   GD Bidding Strategy

Gjerstad and Dickhaut [41] proposed a more sophisticated strategy, called *GD* strategy in this book. A GD agent records all the asks (bids) in the history occurring in the last several rounds. From the history, an agent computes a *subjective belief* of a bid or ask being accepted. The agent can then calculate the *expected utility* of the bid or ask with the following equation:

$$E(x, a) = \begin{cases} p(a)(a - x) & \text{if he is a seller} \\ q(a)(x - a) & \text{if he is a buyer} \end{cases},$$

where x is the reservation price of the unit of the goods, a is the ask or the bid, $p(a)/q(a)$ is the subjective belief of the seller/buyer.

The bid or ask corresponding to the highest expected utility is submitted to the market. By utilizing the subjective belief, the agent is sensitive to the fluctuation of the dynamic market all the time.

For each seller's potential ask a, Gjerstad and Dickhaut define $p(a)$ as the seller's subjective belief that an ask will be accepted by some buyer:

$$p(a) = \frac{\sum_{d \geq a} TA(d) + \sum_{d \geq a} B(d)}{\sum_{d \geq a} TA(d) + \sum_{d \geq a} B(d) + \sum_{d \leq a} RA(d)}. \tag{2.4}$$

Let $TAG(a)=\sum_{d\geq a} TA(d)$, $BG(a)=\sum_{d\geq a} B(d)$, and $RAL(a)=\sum_{d\leq a} RA(d)$. These are the taken asks greater than or equal to a, the bids greater than or equal to a, and the rejected asks less than or equal to a, respectively. Then Equation 2.4 can be rewritten as:

$$p(a) = \frac{TAG(a) + BG(a)}{TAG(a) + BG(a) + RAL(a)}.$$

For each buyer's potential bid b, Gjerstad and Dickhaut define $q(b)$ as the buyer's subjective belief about which bid will be acceptable to some seller:

$$q(b) = \frac{\sum_{d\leq b} TB(d) + \sum_{d\leq b} A(d)}{\sum_{d\leq b} TB(d) + \sum_{d\leq b} A(d) + \sum_{d\geq b} RB(d)}.$$

Let $TBL(b)=\sum_{d\leq b} TB(d)$, $AL(b)=\sum_{d\leq b} A(d)$, and $RBG(b)=\sum_{d\geq b} RB(d)$. These are the taken bids less than or equal to b, the asks less than or equal to b, and the rejected bids greater than or equal to b. Then

$$q(b) = \frac{TBL(b) + AL(b)}{TBL(b) + AL(b) + RBG(b)}.$$

The belief functions are defined on the set of all asks and bids within the trader's memory. These beliefs can be extended to the positive reals using cubic spline interpolation [41].

Tesauro and Das [108] proposed some improvements to the GD algorithm. A principal limitation is that they assume that the demand and supply do not fluctuate over time. Their assumption is not valid in practical CDA markets, where supply and demand constantly change due to the changing economic condition.

Tesauro and Bredin [107] developed a sequential bidding strategy on the basis of dynamic programming in CDAs. They use the belief function together with a forecast of the changes of the beliefs over time. However, the belief function resembles that of GD strategy except for slight modifications.

2.3.5 A-FL Bidding Strategy

He, Leung, and Jennings [53] proposed the *FL* strategy, which first introduces fuzzy sets and fuzzy reasoning into the heuristic rules for agents. A fuzzy logic-based approach can cope with uncertainties in a timely manner. An FL seller or buyer calculates an ask or a bid by considering the relationship among the outstanding bid, the outstanding ask, and the reference price P_R. The FL-strategy is based on a number of heuristic rules and the fuzzy reasoning mechanism. If the relation of P_R, oa, and ob during a round in a CDA falls into one of the cases, the ask or bid is calculated in different ways, shown in Figures 2.7 and 2.8.

A-FL strategy [53] is an adaptive version of the FL strategy. If a seller agent or a buyer agent waits too long to conduct a deal, it means that he should be

---

1: **if** $P_R \leq ob < oa$ **then**

2:     **if** (ob is much_bigger than P_R) **then**

3:         accept ob;

4:     **else**

5:         ask is $(oa - \beta_{s,1}, \theta, \chi)$;

6:     **end if**

7: **end if**

8: **if** $ob < oa \leq P_R$ **then**

9:     **if** (oa is much_smaller than P_R) **then**

10:         no new ask;

11:     **else**

12:         ask is $(oa - \beta_{s,2}, \theta, \chi)$;

13:     **end if**

14: **end if**

15: **if** $ob \leq P_R \leq oa$ **then**

16:     **if** (ob is far_from or medium_to P_R) and (oa is far_from P_R) **then**

17:         ask is $(oa - \lambda_{s,1}, \theta, \chi)$;

18:     **end if**

19:     **if** (ob is far_from or medium_to P_R) and (oa is medium_to P_R) **then**

20:         ask is $(oa - \lambda_{s,2}, \theta, \chi)$;

21:     **end if**

22:     **if** (ob is far_from or medium_to P_R) and (oa is close_to P_R) **then**

23:         ask is $(oa - \lambda_{s,3}, \theta, \chi)$;

24:     **end if**

25:     **if** (ob is close_to P_R) **then**

26:         ask is $(P_R + \lambda_{s,4}, \theta, \chi)$;

27:     **end if**

28: **end if**

Figure 2.7: The pseudo code of the algorithm for the A-FL sellers.

1: **if** $ob < oa \leq P_R$ **then**
2:    **if** (oa is much_smaller than P_R) **then**
3:       accept oa;
4:    **else**
5:       bid is $(ob + \beta_{b,1}, \theta, \chi)$;
6:    **end if**
7: **end if**
8: **if** $P_R \leq ob < oa$ **then**
9:    **if** (ob is much_bigger than P_R) **then**
10:       no new bid;
11:    **else**
12:       bid is $(ob + \beta_{b,2}, \theta, \chi)$;
13:    **end if**
14: **end if**
15: **if** $ob \leq P_R \leq oa$ **then**
16:    **if** (oa is far_from or medium_to P_R) and (ob is far_from P_R) **then**
17:       bid is $(ob + \lambda_{b,1}, \theta, \chi)$;
18:    **end if**
19:    **if** (oa is far_from or medium_to P_R) and (ob is medium_to P_R) **then**
20:       bid is $(ob + \lambda_{b,2}, \theta, \chi)$;
21:    **end if**
22:    **if** (oa is far_from or medium_to P_R) and (ob is close_to P_R) **then**
23:       bid is $(ob + \lambda_{b,3}, \theta, \chi)$;
24:    **end if**
25:    **if** (oa is close_to P_R) **then**
26:       bid is $(P_R - \lambda_{b,4}, \theta, \chi)$;
27:    **end if**
28: **end if**

Figure 2.8: The pseudo code of the algorithm for the A-FL buyers.

1: **if** agent i waits_long to transact **then**
2:      $A^i_{attitude} = A^i_{attitude} - r\wp$;
3: **end if**
4: **if** agent i transacts_frequently **then**
5:      $A^i_{attitude} = A^i_{attitude} + r\wp$;
6: **end if**

Figure 2.9: The learning rules for A-FL agents.

more risk averse in the next round if he is going to make more transactions. On the contrary, if a seller agent or a buyer agent can transact very frequently, it is a sign that his bids/asks are too high/low. Thus, during the next round of the CDA, the agent should change his attitude in the direction of risk-seeking, hoping he can still make a transaction while increasing his profit. This kind of hill-climbing behaviour is the learning rule of the A-FL agent, shown in Figure 2.9. Through updating the risk attitude of the agent, the value of β and λ in Figures 2.7 and 2.8 will be adjusted step by step, and consequently the value of the ask or bid to be submitted. This adaptivity helps the agent earn more profit from the market.

2.3.6   Other Bidding Strategies

P-strategy [86] was designed by Park *et al.* P-strategy is developed based on stochastic modeling for a CDA. The idea of the P-strategy is to model the auction process with a Markov Chain (MC). However, it is hard to acquire the probability values for the MC model, such as the transition probabilities and the probabilities of success and failure for trading actions. In addition, the computation involved in this approach is huge.

A risk-based strategy is proposed by Vytelingum *et al.* [116]. The strategy involves an agent's forming a bid or ask by assessing the degree of risk involved and making a prediction about the competitive equilibrium that is likely to be reached in the marketplace. The agents adapt their risk attitude (risk-averse, risk-neutral, and risk-seeking) based on their past experience. The moving average method is adopted to estimate the competitive equilibrium price according to the history of transactions. However, the moving average method is only sensitive to price changes over a short time frame, not over a long time span.

Li and Smith [63] presented an agent-based framework of B2B exchanges in the context of continuous double auctions. In multiple periods of continuous double auctions, the demand or supply changes from period to period, which causes price fluctuation. It is price fluctuation that motivates users to accumulate inventory. Hence, speculation inventory is introduced which enables a buyer to purchase more products than current needs to cut future purchase costs, while a seller may keep extra products on hand and in expectation of selling at a higher price in the future.

2.3.7 Discussion

Although all the bidding strategies obey the basic protocol of CDAs, many differences exist in each specific rule and factor considered in the strategies. The following factors are usually considered by one or more of these bidding strategies.

- A history of transaction prices: For an agent, if he has been involved in the trading for several consecutive rounds, he can save all the transaction prices into an array for his future use. This array is a history of transaction prices.

- The outstanding ask and the outstanding bid: In one CDA market, the current lowest ask is called the outstanding ask while the current highest bid is called the outstanding bid.

- Reservation prices: There is a reservation price for each unit of goods per agent. For a seller, if the ask he submitted is lower than the reservation price of the unit of goods, he will lose money. Similarly, for a buyer, if the bid he submitted is higher than the reservation price, he will lose money as well.

- Reference price: The *reference price* was introduced by He *et al.* [53]. It refers to the median in a series of transaction prices of several consecutive rounds.

- The transaction price of the last round: If there was a transaction in the last round, then the agent can record the transaction price as a guide to the possible transaction price in the current market.

- The combination of sellers or buyers: In one CDA market, there are multiple buyers and multiple sellers. Each buyer or seller may adopt different bidding strategies. Therefore, the combination of sellers or buyers means the distribution of how many sellers/buyers use strategy A, how many use strategy B, or C, *etc.* In real-life markets, the combination of sellers or buyers is not publicly known.

- The risk attitude of an agent: *Risk attitude* is a spectrum of various attitudes towards risk from most risk-seeking to most risk-averse [53], [64], [116]. For a risk-seeking agent, he prefers the risk of not achieving a successful transaction to a guaranteed success. For a risk-averse agent, he prefers the opposite choice. If not risk-seeking or risk-averse, it is risk-neutral.

- The forecast of future market situations: It mainly refers to the anticipation of future transaction prices, future supply and demand relationships, *etc.*

Nevertheless we find that some factors, such as softness of asks or bids, judgement of price acceptability, and time strategies, are seldom taken into consideration by the above strategies in the literature. As we shall demonstrate in this book, these factors can greatly enhance the performance of the strategies. Therefore these three factors should be under consideration and we introduce them one by one in the following:

- Softness of soft asks or bids: Normally, an agent will compute an ask or a bid which is a determined value. However, for a soft ask or bid, there are a determined value and a range with which the agent can make compromise. This range is the softness of soft asks or bids.

- Judgement of price acceptability: For an agent who has the ability to judge the acceptable price, he will set some thresholds to asks or bids in the market. For instance, as a seller agent, if the current *ob* is higher than one threshold, it means the *ob* is profitable enough and he will accept the bid immediately. For a seller, the value of this threshold decreases with difficulty in trading.

- Time strategies: When the CDA market employs a fixed deadline to terminate each round, time strategies are introduced for agents in the market to arrange his behaviour according to time.

2.4   Evaluation Criteria of Bidding Strategies

The main criterion to evaluate the performance of a bidding strategy is profit or utility. The higher the profit or utility, the better the performance. Among all types of auctions, there are dominant strategies for some auctions and for others there are not. For some auctions with dominant strategies, it is feasible to analyze the performance of an agent using a game theoretical approach. For example, in SPSB auctions, the dominant strategy is to submit the true reservation price [114], [78], [97], [14]. In English auctions, the agent's dominant strategy is to bid a small amount more than the current highest bid while the bid does not exceed the agent's reservation price [62], [76], [97], [45]. For SPSB and English auctions, the one whose true reservation price is the highest will win the auction. His profit is or almost equals the difference between the highest and the second highest reservation prices.

However, for those auctions where there are no dominant strategies, it is hard to analyze the performance. For example, in Dutch auctions, FPSB auctions, and continuous double auctions, there is no dominant bidding strategy [74] [77] [97]. Therefore a theoretical approach cannot work to analyze the performance of agents.

To evaluate the performance of an agent in these auctions in a meaningful way, specific laboratorial market environments should be designed, which simulate markets in real life. Normally, two kinds of trading environments need to be considered. The simple and conventional kind is static market environment, in which the same traders are required to join every round and not allowed to leave the market freely. The more complex kind is a dynamic market environment. Traders in this dynamic market are allowed to join or leave the market at any moment, which causes the combination of sellers and/or buyers to be changed and the supply and demand relationship to fluctuate accordingly. If an agent demonstrates a good performance in both kinds of laboratorial markets, the overall performance of the agent is demonstrated to be good.

2.5   Approaches for Analyzing Bidding Strategies

There are mainly four kinds of approaches to analyzing the performance of agents using various biding strategies, *i.e.*, experimental approaches, game theoretic approaches, empirical game theoretic approaches, and evolutionary approaches, which are discussed in turn below.

2.5.1   Experimental Approaches

An experimental approach is a main method utilized to analyze the performance of a bidding strategy in continuous double auctions. There are two parts to pay attention to: the experimental setup and the market environments simulated. From previous work in the literature [101], [42], [41], [92], [22], [53], [116], [63], we know these two parts are key issues when designing experiments.

In the experimental setup, designers should consider the following aspects and specify clearly: the number of sellers/buyers in the market, the bidding strategies for each agent to use, the distribution of reservation prices for each agent, the clearing policy of the market, the evaluation criteria of agents' performance, the duration time for each round, privacy of information, and so on.

To design a laboratorial market environment for agents to trade in, designers may focus on the following perspectives: the number of rounds of transactions that should be conducted, employing static markets and/or dynamic markets, using sequential or simultaneous auctions, the reset of the experimental setup at the beginning of each round, *etc.* After determining these perspectives, a specific experimental market environment can be built and the performance of agents can be evaluated in the laboratorial market.

The advantages of experimental approaches are that experimental approaches are quick to make a start; there is little limitation of the strategies agents adopt; there are also few limitations on the market environment and auction protocols; it is easy to simulate dynamic markets; the profit of agents can be calculated without effort. Given these advantages, experimental approaches are especially suitable to analyze many types of auctions where there is no dominant strategy. Therefore, this approach is widely adopted in the research area of continuous double auctions.

Certainly, there are some disadvantages of experimental approaches as well. The most obvious one is that one can never carry out all types of experiments to simulate all different market environments, especially when there are large numbers of possible strategies, or a large population of agents. Therefore, when one chooses this approach, one should pay attention to the following aspects. First, one needs to select the representative experimental environments. Second, one needs to select the representative parameters in such environments. Third, one needs to determine which parameters are to be varied in which market environments. Finally the trend of the target parameters in different market environments can be detected if one's aim is to explore the general rules for these parameters. Or the performance of various strategies can be compared thoroughly if one's aim is to draw a conclusion on which strategy performs best in which environment. This whole procedure will help the experimental results to be more meaningful.

2.5.2   Game Theoretic Analysis Approaches

Game theory is a source of stability criteria often employed in multi-agent systems (MAS) research. Game theory provides a rigorous mathematical framework for formalizing interactions among rational agents. Game theory pays attention to equilibria in systems or equilibrium from the perspective of whole systems, rather than emphasizing the target agent's utility or profit.

However, in our work, our focus is on enhancing the profit of the target agent and we do not care about enhancing the profit of the other agents or the equilibrium of the system. If our target agent can grab more profit from other agents in the market, it will demonstrate the usefulness of our proposed tools or strategies. Therefore, to analyze the equilibria in or equilibrium of systems is not our interest in this book.

2.5.3   Empirical Game Theoretic Analysis Approaches

Over the past few years, Wellman *et al.* [123] have been developing an experimental methodology for explicit game-theoretic treatment of MAS simulation studies, which is referred to as empirical game-theoretic analysis.

An empirical game-theoretic analysis of agent strategies is composed of the following steps:

1. Approximate the original trading market in the form of a game by several agents as players of the game.

2. Run many simulations covering all distinct strategy profiles for each agent.

3. Process the simulation data by checking game validity and adjusting for stochastic demand variability.

4. Analyze the resulting empirical game by searching for equilibria and approximate equilibria.

Finally pure strategy equilibria, mixed strategy equilibria, symmetric equilibrium, Nash equilibrium, or approximate equilibrium can be analyzed. These results help researchers understand more of complex multi-agent systems. [2]

However, several disadvantages show up. The data set of game instances is very large. Therefore, if there are many agents trading in the auction market, then it is almost impossible to carry out each profile of strategies. Accordingly, if not all possible profiles or not all market environments are tested, some equilibria may

---

[2]Wellman *et al.* also point out in their paper [123] that currently their work only focuses on several agents with a small number of strategies. Further development and other techniques need to be researched for this newly proposed approach to be practical.

not be found. Moreover, this approach aims to detect the existence of equilibrium or equilibria of the whole system, which we repeat is not our interest in this book.

2.5.4 Evolutionary Approaches

Perhaps the most popular approach to determining a relevant population of agent strategies is an appeal to evolutionary methods. The evolutionary approach was pioneered in computational agent research by Axelrod [3], and has become a standard method among researchers in agent-based computational economics. Techniques for strategy generation are typically based on genetic algorithms or genetic programming [79], [16], [19], [18].

The disadvantage of evolutionary approaches is that training data and training processes are necessary and crucial for the later practical auction markets. In our work for this book, laboratorial markets are designed to simulate real-life markets where there is no such training period for any agent. All the agents are put into the experiments and are allowed to compete with each other. In this way, the laboratorial market is fair for all agents and simulates more of the market in real life.

2.5.5 Approaches Adopted in this Book

The laboratorial auction market considered in this book has several features. First, the market has a limited number of agents trading simultaneously in the market. Therefore, individual behaviour will affect market performance. Second, some information is public while some is private. For example, the values of oa and ob are publicly known; the values of reservation prices for each unit of goods of different agents are private information. Third, different agents use different bidding strategies and there are no dominant strategy. Fourth, the market is dynamic since the supply and demand relationship is changing and the combination of agents is also changing. Fifth, the laboratorial market has no training period or mock trading period (this resembles more of real-life markets). Finally, the aim of the experiments is to evaluate the performance of the target agent by computing profit.

Given these features and the aim, the game theoretic approach and the empirical game theoretic approach are not suitable in that our interest is in analyzing the performance of target agent instead of all the agents in the system; nevertheless they are interested in analyzing the equilibrium of the whole system including all the agents. The evolutionary approach cannot be adopted by reason of the training period it requires. The training period is not available in our laboratorial market which aims to resemble real-life markets.

We choose experimental approaches because this approach gives a way to directly compare various bidding strategies in dynamic and practical environments. The effects of various strategy design components can be observed through a series of markets with different parameter values. It also enables us to simulate the trading environment of real-life markets.

The design of bidding strategies often includes many components that are not easily captured by an game theoretic analysis. Instead, they are inspired by and based on experience and domain knowledge provided by human traders; hence they provide a more appropriate basis for automation and can be used in a wider variety of application domains. Such design components of bidding strategies are not based on formal theories and it is difficult to analyze them formally. The experimental approaches can delve deeper into evaluating the overall performance of different bidding strategies and have become the *de facto* standard approaches for evaluation of bidding strategies in the research community of intelligent agents.

One example of such design components is the introduction of softness of asks or bids, that provides a range for an agent to make compromise. We show, in Chapter 4, that if the current market favors the agent, he can trade all his goods and should not make compromises; if the market is against the agent, he cannot have many transactions and should make compromises in return for more transactions. Therefore, the pre-requisite to efficiently employ softness of asks or bids is that the agent has to know the market situation, *i.e.*, whether it is easy or difficult for him to trade. Agents employing the proposed AA strategy sense the environment and are able to perceive signals to determine the market situation and make appropriate decisions. It is obvious that it is difficult to formally analyze such design components, but their effectiveness can be clearly shown by experiments simulating different market conditions.

Another example is the use of the long-term and short-term eagerness in decision making. If we take a look at human traders in the market, we can observe that human traders often have some kind of subjective feelings along with the trading process in a short period and a long period as well. For example, human traders will feel eager for more profit when they find that they have lots of transactions. Otherwise they may feel eager for more transactions if they have very few transactions. This feeling, called eagerness in this book, reflects the market supply and demand relationship from the human trader's own point of view and suitable for acting as the signal for the traders on whether it is easy or difficult for them to trade. Guided by the signal, agents can explore the market situation from time to time and adapt softness of asks or bids, judgement of price acceptability, and time strategies with the dynamic market. When the market environment or the bidding strategy can hardly be formally modeled, experiments can still be designed and bidding strategies can be implemented and evaluated.

The disadvantage of this approach is that one can never carry out all types of experiments to simulate all types of market environments, especially when there are a large numbers of possible strategies or variants. Even when it is feasible to carry out a large number of experiments, the analyst must be careful to interpret the experimental results and point out the limitation brought by the various parameters and assumptions in order to draw conclusions about proposed strategies. Therefore the obtained conclusions cannot be guaranteed to be generally applicable for different or untried market environments.

Chapter 3

The Adaptive Attitude Bidding Strategy

In this chapter, we develop a novel *Adaptive Attitude (AA)* bidding strategy that agents can use to participate in CDAs. The AA strategy exploits both the short-term and long-term attitudes of an agent, and utilizes a threshold-based method with heuristic rules (called the α-ω method) in bid determination. Eagerness is defined for the first time. The effectiveness of the strategy is demonstrated by empirically benchmarking it against the main strategies that have been proposed in the literature and this evaluation shows that the AA strategy is superior in a wide range of market situations.

The remainder of this chapter is organized as follows. Section 3.1 introduces eagerness and proposes an eagerness function to compute the value of eagerness. Section 3.2 presents the AA strategy. In Section 3.3, the performance of agents employing AA strategy is evaluated in experiments. Section 3.4 concludes this chapter.

Part of the material presented in this chapter has been published in [73], [67].

3.1 Eagerness

3.1.1 Eagerness in Agent Interactions

The core of the adaptive attitude is eagerness which has been defined independently by several pieces of work. Sim defines eagerness as a measure of an agent's interest in negotiating and coming to a deal [100]. It models the intensity of the need to acquire the goods under negotiation. The level of interest may be categorized as: must deal, desirable, nice to have, optional, unessential, and absolutely unessential. The value of eagerness is always specified by human negotiators before the experiments begin. During each experiment, the value is constant.

Dumas *et al.* [27], [28] propose an eagerness factor which represents the minimum probability of obtaining the goods by the deadline. The eagerness factor is a measure of an agent's risk attitude. A low eagerness value means that the agent is willing to take the risk of not getting the unit of goods by the deadline, if this can allow the agent to find a better price. An eagerness value close to 1 means that the agent wants to get the unit of goods by the deadline at any price if the reservation price permits. However, the value of eagerness is also fixed and unfluctuating with the market situation.

Later, several pieces of work mention a similar idea about eagerness. Vytelingum *et al.* [115] define the aggressiveness of the bidding behaviour as how eager an agent is to transact. They consider three types of bidding behaviour: neutral, passive, and aggressive. Their aim is to explore what type of behaviour should be adopted given the particular population distribution of types. Nevertheless, such population distribution is rarely known in a dynamic market.

Goyal *et al.* [44] propose that in a dynamic multi-agent world, the behaviour of an agent is based on appropriate commitment of the agent to all unexpected situations in the world. The agent needs to know how weak or strong the commitment is if he is committed to executing his action. The agent thus needs to know the degree of his commitment towards the action. This degree of commitment quantifies the agent's attitude towards the action execution. The attitude, once adopted, must persist for a reasonable period of time so that other agents can use it to predict the behaviour of the agent under consideration, which is not applicable for the dynamic CDA market.

The eagerness defined in this book is not a constant during the experiments. Instead, the value changes with the dynamic market environment and is affected by the realtime supply and demand relationship from the agent's own point of view, which makes it a meaningful indicator for the agent's attitude in the market.

3.1.2 Eagerness Function for Agents in CDAs

Eagerness should be affected by an agent's feeling in the past several rounds and in the last run. In the past several rounds of the current run, if the agent achieved a lot of transactions, he will be eager for more profit in the next rounds. On the contrary, he will be eager for more transactions in the next rounds. However, the transaction situation in the current run alone is not enough, considering there are multiple consecutive runs of CDAs. The agent's feeling in the current run will be affected by his transaction situation in the last run as well. If the agent had a good transaction record in the last run, this will encourage him to be eager for more profit in the current run. Otherwise, if he had very few transactions in the last run, he will be eager for more transactions in the current run. Since several rounds of time is a short time when compared with a run, we call the feeling formed during several rounds *short-term attitude*. We call the feeling developed during a run *long-term attitude*. In this book, we propose one possible way to express eagerness.

Before we present eagerness and bidding strategies, two important definitions of eagerness are given first.

Definition 3.1.1. Let $NUM_{W=I}$ be the number of successful transactions in the past r rounds in which agent i is the winner. NUM_{total} is the total number of successful transactions in the past r rounds. The *transaction rate* T_i^r is calculated by:

$$T_i^r = NUM_{W=I} \div NUM_{total}.$$

Definition 3.1.2. Let $NUNIT_{traded}$ be the number of agent i's units traded successfully in the last run. $NUNIT_{owned}$ is the total number of units agent i wanted to trade in the last run. The *transaction percentage* $T_{p,i}$ is defined as:

$$T_{p,i} = NUNIT_{traded} \div NUNIT_{owned}.$$

The eagerness function is built on the foundation of two attitudes: the short-term attitude and the long-term attitude. The function represents the feeling of the agent in a series of CDAs. As a seller, a high value of the function represents that the seller is eager to gain more profit by selling each unit of goods at high prices. A low value of the function represents that the seller is eager to make more transactions. Similarly, for a buyer, a high value of the function demonstrates that the buyer is eager for more profit. A low value demonstrates the buyer is eager for more transactions. The eagerness function is defined as follows:

$$F_{eager}(T_i^r, T_{p,i}) = T_i^r \times A(T_{p,i}) \times W(T_i^r).$$

T_i^r represents the *short-term attitude* which is related to a period of a few consecutive rounds. $W(T_i^r)$ is the weight of the short-term attitude. $W(T_i^r)$ is an increasing function for sellers and buyers and computed by Equation 3.1. W_1, W_2, and W_3 are different positive values of weight. W_1 is smaller than W_2 and W_2 is smaller than W_3 which are specified at the beginning of a round. If an agent feels that he makes transactions too often, he will be eager for more profit and the value of T_i^r is large. Under this situation, the eagerness function will return a high value with a high weight and a large T_i^r.

$$W(T_i^r) = \begin{cases} W_1 \times T_i^r & \text{small } T_i^r \\ W_2 \times T_i^r & \text{medium } T_i^r \\ W_3 \times T_i^r & \text{large } T_i^r \end{cases} . \qquad (3.1)$$

$T_{p,i}$ represents the *long-term attitude* . $A(T_{p,i})$ is the weight of the long-term attitude. In a series of CDAs, any seller or buyer can compare successive runs and remember useful information from previous runs. As a seller, if he has sold all the units he wanted to sell in the last run, he would be eager for more profit in the current run. In this case, the eagerness function should return a high value. The seller believes that he has left a lot of profit for buyers in the last run and he should increase his asks on each unit of goods in the current run and grab more profit back from buyers. Otherwise, the seller should be willing to decrease his prices and eager for more transactions in the current run. The eagerness function should return a low value. $A(T_{p,i})$[1] is calculated in the following equation:

$$A(T_{p,i}) = \begin{cases} A + \delta & T_{p,i} = 1.0 \\ A - \delta & T_{p,i} < 1.0 \end{cases},$$

where δ is a small positive real number. A is a positive real number specified at the beginning of a round. The computation of $A(T_{p,i})$ for buyers is similar to that of sellers.

Definition 3.1.3. Eagerness is the value computed by $F_{eager}(T_i^r, T_{p,i})$.

3.2 Bidding Strategies Based on Eagerness

In this section, we utilize a threshold-based method with heuristic rules (called the α-ω method) in bid determination for sellers and buyers. In the bidding strategies for sellers, if ob is higher than or equal to ω, the seller will think it is quite profitable and accept the ob; if oa is lower than α, the seller will think that the current market is not profitable at all and submit no new ask. Similarly, in the bidding strategies for buyers, there are two thresholds α and ω as well. If ob is higher than ω, the buyer will think that the current market is not profitable at all and submit no new bid; if oa is lower than or equal to α, the buyer will think it is quite profitable and accept the oa at once.

3.2.1 The Bidding Strategy for Sellers

We divide one round into three phases. The first phase is the beginning of the round when there is no ob or oa. The second phase is when there is either ob or oa. The third phase is when there are both ob and oa.

Suppose seller i is selling the kth unit in a round. In the first phase of the round, the seller has no information other than the reservation price C_{ik} of unit k and the acceptable price range of the CDA market. The seller tends to submit a high ask and computes his ask as follows:

$$ask = C_{ik} + (P_{ul} - C_{ik}) \times R1,$$

where R1 is a random real number.[2]

When there is only either ob or oa in the market, the seller will utilize ob or oa to compute his ask. If there is ob and no oa, the seller will use the following equation:

---

[1] If the number of the units of goods is very large, $T_{p,i}$ is not necessarily equal to 1.0. $T_{p,i}$, less than 1.0, is acceptable.

[2] For example, R1 can be located in $[0.85, 1.0]$ to obtain higher asks.

$$\text{ask} = \begin{cases} ob & ob \geq \omega \\ ob + (P_{ul} - ob) \times F_{eager} & ob < \omega \text{ and } ob > C_{ik} \\ C_{ik} + (P_{ul} - C_{ik}) \times F_{eager} & ob < \omega \text{ and } ob \leq C_{ik} \end{cases},$$

where F_{eager} represents the feeling of eagerness of the agent. ω is a threshold in the α-ω method for sellers. If ob is higher than or equal to ω, the seller will submit an ask equal to ob. Otherwise, the seller will compute an ask according to his feeling of eagerness. The new ask must be higher than the reservation price C_{ik} in case of losing profit. At the same time, the ask must be higher than the current ob because ob is not high enough. If the current ob is higher than C_{ik}, the new ask will be calculated by $ob + (P_{ul} - ob) \times F_{eager}$. If not, the new ask will be calculated by $C_{ik} + (P_{ul} - C_{ik}) \times F_{eager}$.

If there is oa and no ob in the round, the seller will calculate his new ask according to oa. If oa is lower than α which is another threshold in the α-ω method for sellers, the seller will submit no new ask. Otherwise, the seller will give a new ask slightly lower than the current oa.

In the third phase, both oa and ob exist in the market. If ob is higher than or equal to ω, the seller will submit an ask equal to ob. If oa is lower than α, the seller will submit no new ask. If oa is not too low and ob is not so high, the seller will compute his ask according to his eagerness. The seller computes the basic price and target price, denoted as P_{basic} and P_{target} respectively. If there was a transaction in the last round, the seller would take the maximum of the transaction price and the outstanding bid as the target price. If there was no transaction in the last run, the seller would take the maximum of the last outstanding ask and the outstanding bid as the target price. The basic price is given by the following:

$$P_{basic} = C_{ik} \times R2,$$

where R2 is initially a random real number.[3]

If there was a successful transaction in the last round, the seller would employ the following equation to calculate the target price:

$$P_{target} = \max(P_{t\_last} + \theta, ob_{current}),$$

where θ is a small random positive real number, $ob_{current}$ is the current outstanding bid, and P_{t_last} is the transaction price of the last round.

If there was not a transaction in the last round, the seller would employ the following equation:

$$P_{target} = \max(oa_{last} - \beta, ob_{current}),$$

where β is a small random positive real number, oa_{last} is the outstanding ask of the last round.

---

[3] For example, R2 can be located in [1.0, 1.5].

The basic price gives an initial profit for the seller. The target price gives the destination for the seller. The size of the step, denoted as S_{step}, is calculated by the equation below:

$$S_{step} = \begin{cases} (P_{target} - P_{basic}) \times F_{eager} & P_{target} \geq P_{basic} \\ (\max(P_{target}, C_{ik}) - P_{basic}) \times (1 - F_{eager}) & P_{target} < P_{basic} \end{cases}.$$

The final ask is calculated by the equation

$$\text{ask} = P_{basic} + S_{step}.$$

3.2.2   The Bidding Strategy for Buyers

There are also the same three phases in a round for buyers. Suppose buyer j is buying the kth unit in a round. In the first phase, the buyer has no information other than his reservation price R_{jk} of unit k and the acceptable price range of the CDA market. The buyer tends to submit a low bid and computes the bid by the following equation:

$$\text{bid} = R_{jk} - (R_{jk} - P_{ll}) \times R3,$$

where R3 is a random real number.[4]

If there is oa and no ob, the buyer will calculate his bid using the following equation:

$$\text{bid} = \begin{cases} oa & oa \leq \alpha \\ oa - (oa - P_{ll}) \times F_{eager} & oa > \alpha \text{ and } oa \leq R_{jk} \\ R_{jk} - (R_{jk} - P_{ll}) \times F_{eager} & oa > \alpha \text{ and } oa > R_{jk} \end{cases}. \qquad (3.2)$$

α is a threshold in the α-ω method for buyers. If oa is lower than or equal to α, this buyer will think the ask is low enough to be accepted directly. Otherwise, this buyer will compute his new bid by case 2 or case 3 in Equation 3.2.

If there is ob and no oa, the buyer will submit no bid if the current ob is higher than ω, another threshold in the α-ω method for buyers. Otherwise, the buyer will submit his new bid slightly higher than the current ob.

When there are already ob and oa, if the current oa is lower than or equal to α, the buyer will accept the ask directly. If the current ob is higher than ω, this buyer will not submit any new bid. Otherwise the buyer will compute the bid by the following equations.

$$P_{basic} = R_{jk} \times R4,$$

where R4 is initially a random real number.[5]

---

[4]Similarly to R1, R3 can, for instance, be located in $[0.85, 1.0]$.
[5]Similarly to R2, R4 can, for instance, be located in $[0.5, 1.0]$.

If there was a successful transaction in the last round, the buyer would adopt the equation below to calculate the target price:

$$P_{target} = \min(P_{t\_last} - \theta, oa_{current}),$$

where θ is a small random positive real number, $oa_{current}$ is the current outstanding ask, and P_{t_last} is the transaction price of the last round.

If there was not a successful transaction in the last round, the target price would be calculated by the following equation:

$$P_{target} = \min(ob_{last} + \beta, oa_{current}),$$

where β is a small random positive real number, ob_{last} is the outstanding bid of the last round.

$$S_{step} = \begin{cases} (P_{target} - P_{basic}) \times F_{eager} & P_{target} \leq P_{basic} \\ (\min(P_{target}, R_{jk}) - P_{basic}) \times (1 - F_{eager}) & P_{target} > P_{basic} \end{cases}.$$

The final bid is given by the equation

$$\text{bid} = P_{basic} + S_{step}.$$

3.3 Experimental Analysis

We carry out experiments in two groups: experiments to simulate static CDA markets, and experiments to simulate dynamic CDA markets. The ultimate goal of the experiments is to analyze the performance of AA strategy in the dynamic CDA markets which resemble the practical CDA markets where all the sellers or buyers are free to join or leave the market. Through all the experimental results, it is demonstrated that AA strategy performs the best in the dynamic CDA markets.

Our first step is to implement the experiments which simulate static CDA markets. The reason is that the static market is a simple environment compared with the dynamic market. Based on the results of experiments simulating the static CDA markets, AA strategy is demonstrated to be superior to others. Then we begin to implement experiments which simulate dynamic CDA markets. In order to clearly analyze the performance of AA strategy, we particularly design the experiments to compare AA agents and one kind of other agents one by one in dynamic CDA markets. Through the experimental results, AA strategy is observed to outperform any other kind of strategies. Finally, we put AA agents and all the other kinds of agents to compete together in one dynamic CDA market.

3.3.1   Experiments to Simulate Static CDA Markets

The settings of the experiments to simulate static CDA markets are as follows. First, each experiment is composed of multiple 1,000 runs. In each run, a seller is endowed with a number of units of goods, reservation prices of which are independently drawn from a uniform distribution within $[1.0, 1.5]$. A buyer is endowed with a number of units of goods whose reservation prices are independently drawn from a uniform distribution within $[3.0, 3.5]$. In order to compare each kind of agents' profit, we keep the reservation prices of different kinds of agents and the number of units of goods of each kind the same. Second, in order to resemble a human traders' thinking process before submitting his ask or bid to the market, we force the agent to allow a time period to elapse before submitting an ask or a bid. This time period is specified as a randomly distributed variable and called "thinking time" in this book. Third, to measure how well an agent performs in a CDA, we evaluate his profit. For a seller i, the total *profit* on all s units sold in a run is $\sum_{k=1}^{s}(P_{ik} - C_{ik})$, where P_{ik} is the transaction price. Similarly for a buyer j, the total profit on all t units bought in a run is $\sum_{k=1}^{t}(R_{jk} - P_{jk})$ and P_{jk} is the transaction price. In the rest of this chapter, an agent's profit is calculated as the sum of the total profit in 1,000 runs.

Based on the above settings, we compare AA strategy with ZI-U, ZI-C, ZIP, GD, A-FL, and CP strategies. These strategies represent the most widely cited strategies in the literature for agents participating in CDAs. The experiments are carried out to test seven kinds of sellers and seven kinds of buyers respectively. To evaluate the behaviour of each kind of sellers or buyers, we compare their profits in three situations: supply equal to demand (Figures 3.1 and 3.2), supply larger than demand (Figures 3.4 and 3.5), and supply less than demand (Figures 3.3 and 3.6).

In each figure, the horizontal axis shows the supply or demand quantity and the vertical axis shows the profit of agents using different strategies. Each curve represents the profit of one kind of agents. The higher the profit, the better the performance of this kind of agents.

In the experiments for sellers, each kind of sellers has 4 to 10 units of goods to sell. The buyers are all ZI-C agents in order to be fair for seven kinds of sellers. Because all kinds of sellers have the same number of units of goods to trade in every run out of 1000 runs, the combination of sellers is always the same. This means that all the sellers are not allowed to freely join or leave the market as they want. As to the experiment setup for buyers, it is similar to that of the sellers.

The performance of the other six strategies is statistically worse than that of AA agents. ZIP agents behave worse than AA agents because they do not consider the adaptivity in several consecutive rounds. CP agents resemble ZIP agents. GD agents show worse behaviour than AA agents because they focus on the history without considering the transaction price of the last round, the outstanding ask, and the outstanding bid in the current round. ZI-U and ZI-C agents submit random asks and bids, which prevent them from achieving a high profit. A-FL agents can

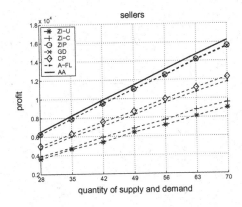

Figure 3.1: Performance of seven different sellers in static markets. The supply equals the demand, increasing from 28 to 70.

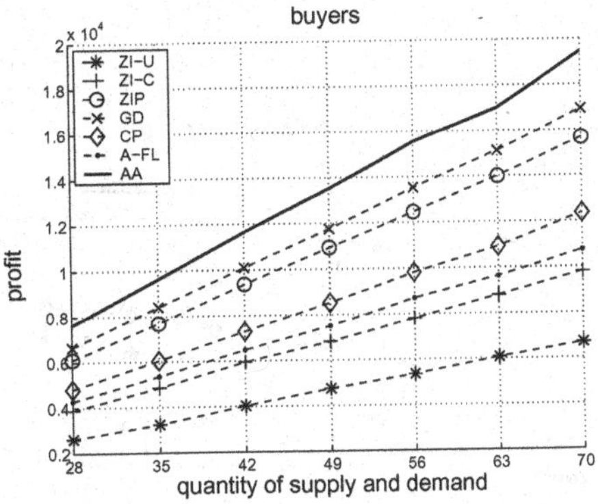

Figure 3.2: Performance of seven different buyers in static markets. The supply equals the demand, increasing from 28 to 70.

be adaptive while they do not consider the long-term adaptivity. As a result, their performance is not as good as that of AA agents.

In order to analyze how the long-term attitude affects the whole performance of AA agents, we design an additional set of experiments. We denote AA without the long-term attitude as AA-NL. In the experiment for sellers, there are eight kinds of sellers, ZI-U, ZI-C, ZIP, GD, A-FL, CP, AA, and AA-NL. The buyers are all ZI-C agents. During each experiment, the number of units of goods and the distribution of reservation prices for these units are kept the same for all kinds of sellers. The number of units of ZI-C buyers changes randomly every 100 runs, which leads to fluctuation of the supply and demand relationship in 1000 runs. Similarly, we implement the experiment to compare the performance of AA buyers and that of AA-NL buyers. Figures 3.7 and 3.8 demonstrate that AA agents gain more profit than AA-NL agents.

3.3.2 Experiments to Simulate Dynamic CDA Markets

In the experiments to simulate static CDA markets, AA agents show a superior performance than other agents. Nevertheless, in practical and dynamic CDA markets, the combination of sellers or buyers fluctuates from time to time because agents can join or leave the market at any moment, which causes the supply and demand relationship to be changed accordingly. Furthermore, one bidding strategy that succeeds in one specific environment may not work well in other environments. For all the above reasons, the following experiments are designed in order to compare the performance of AA strategy with others in the practical and dynamic CDA markets.

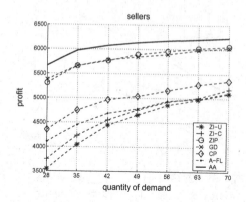

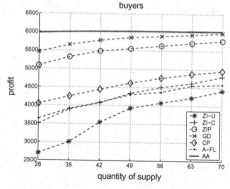

Figure 3.3: Performance of seven different sellers in static markets. The supply is 24. The demand increases from 28 to 70.

Figure 3.4: Performance of seven different buyers in static markets. The supply increases from 28 to 70. The demand is 24.

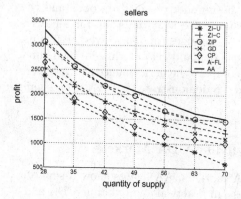

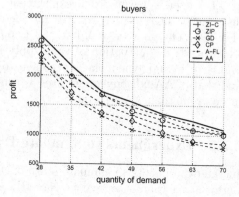

Figure 3.5: Performance of seven different sellers in static markets. The supply increases from 28 to 70. The demand is 24.

Figure 3.6: Performance of six different buyers in static markets. The supply is 24. The demand increases from 28 to 70.

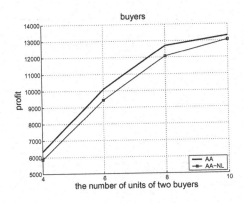

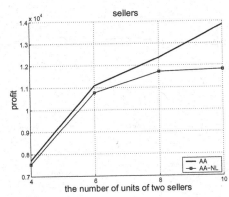

Figure 3.7: Performance of AA buyers and AA-NL buyers.

Figure 3.8: Performance of AA sellers and AA-NL sellers.

Experiments to compare two kinds of agents

To simulate a practical and dynamic CDA market, the experiment setup is as follows. In the experiments for sellers, a group of both AA sellers and one kind of other sellers in comparison each have 5 units of goods to sell. Another group of sellers are selected randomly from a pool which consists of 70 sellers. In this pool, there are 10 AA, 10 ZI-U, 10 ZI-C, 10 ZIP, 10 GD, 10 CP, and 10 A-FL sellers, each of which has one unit of goods to sell. Therefore, except that the two kinds of sellers in comparison must have the same number of units of goods in every run, the group of all other sellers are composed of different kinds of sellers with different total numbers. Consequently, the combination of sellers changes with every run. This can simulate that some sellers are free to join or leave the market as they want, except for the two kinds in comparison. The buyers are all ZI-C buyers in order to be fair to different kinds of sellers.

Following the experiments to simulate static CDA markets, we also divide the supply and demand relationships into supply larger than demand, supply equal to demand, and supply less than demand. For the case of supply larger than demand, at the beginning of every run, the rest of the sellers are selected randomly from a pool with number larger than 40. Thus the total number of units of goods desired to be traded by all sellers is larger than 50. Every 1000 runs, the number of units desired to be bought by buyers is changed from 10, 20, 30, 40, to 50, which is kept smaller than the supply. Similarly, for the case of supply less than demand, the rest of the sellers are selected randomly at the beginning of every run with number smaller than 40. Therefore the supply is always smaller than 50. The number of units of goods desired by buyers is changed from 60, 70, 80, 90, to 100 every 1000 runs, which is larger than the supply. Finally for the case of supply equal to demand, the number of units of goods desired by the rest of the sellers randomly

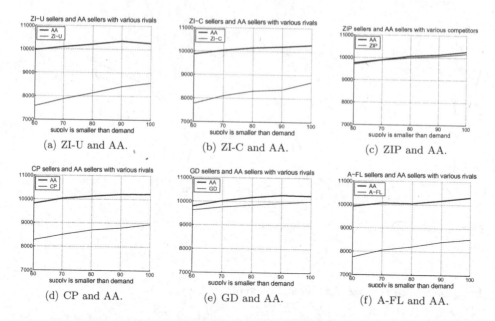

Figure 3.9: The comparison of performance of different sellers with AA sellers in dynamic CDA markets when supply is smaller than demand. The X axis represents demand from 60 to 100. The Y axis represents the profit of two sellers.

selected in each run is changed from 10, 20, 30, 40, to 50 every 1000 runs, while the number of units of goods desired by the buyers is kept the same as that of all the sellers. In the experiments for the buyers, the setup is similar to that of the sellers.

From Figures 3.9, 3.10, 3.11, 3.12, 3.13, and 3.14, it can be seen that the performance of AA agents is always superior to any other kind of agents in the dynamic CDA markets. This demonstrates that (1) AA agents are adaptive to different combinations of competitors; (2) AA agents are adaptive to different supply and demand relationships. ZI-U and ZI-C agents behave worse because they do not analyze the environment and the other agents whom they are competing with. ZIP and GD agents always show a good performance. ZIP agents make use of many factors of the CDA market, such as the transaction price of the last round, the outstanding ask or the outstanding bid of the last round, the profit margin, *etc.* In addition, ZIP agents use an updating rule in machine learning to be adaptive to dynamic environments. However, for ZIP sellers, they do not consider the long-term history longer than one round. They just pay attention to the information of the last round. CP agents behave worse than ZIP agents. GD agents record a neither too long nor too short history and submit the ask or bid that maximizes the expected utility. GD agents can utilize the past successful asks and bids of all

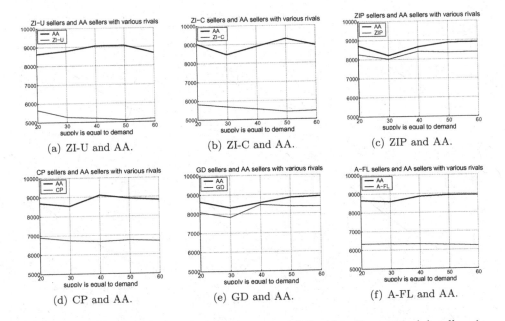

Figure 3.10: The comparison of performance of different sellers with AA sellers in dynamic CDA markets when supply is equal to demand. The X axis represents demand from 20 to 60. The Y axis represents the profit of two sellers.

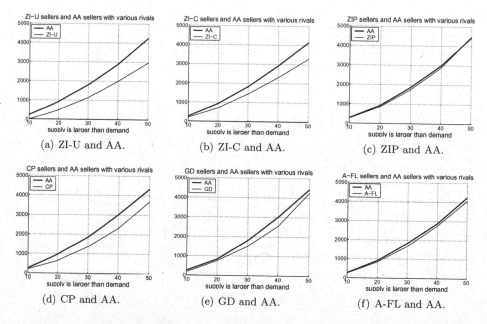

(a) ZI-U and AA.   (b) ZI-C and AA.   (c) ZIP and AA.

(d) CP and AA.   (e) GD and AA.   (f) A-FL and AA.

Figure 3.11: The comparison of performance of different sellers with AA sellers in dynamic CDA markets when supply is larger than demand. The X axis represents demand from 10 to 50. The Y axis represents the profit of two sellers.

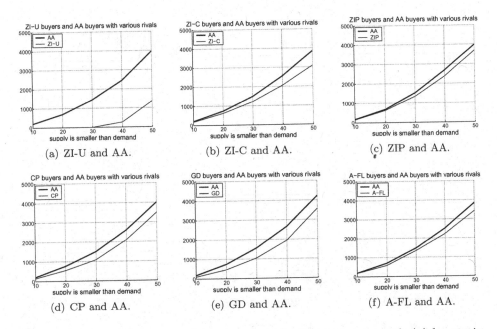

Figure 3.12: The comparison of performance of different buyers with AA buyers in dynamic CDA markets when supply is smaller than demand. The X axis represents supply from 10 to 50. The Y axis represents the profit of two buyers.

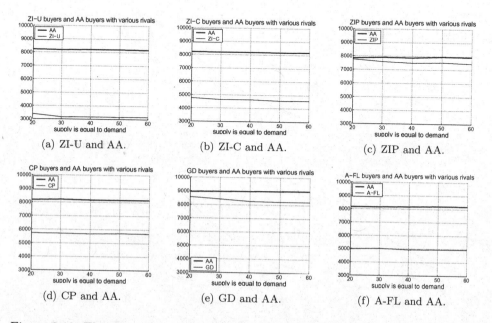

(a) ZI-U and AA.   (b) ZI-C and AA.   (c) ZIP and AA.

(d) CP and AA.   (e) GD and AA.   (f) A-FL and AA.

Figure 3.13: The comparison of performance of different buyers with AA buyers in dynamic CDA markets when supply is equal to demand. The X axis represents supply from 20 to 60. The Y axis represents the profit of two buyers.

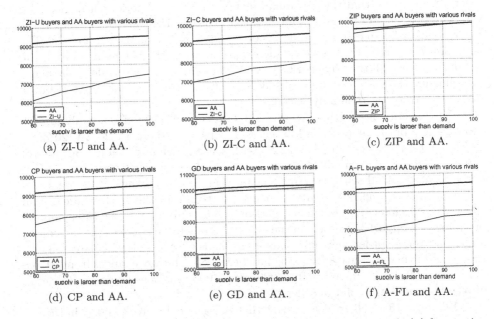

Figure 3.14: The comparison of performance of different buyers with AA buyers in dynamic CDA markets when supply is larger than demand. The X axis represents supply from 60 to 100. The Y axis represents the profit of two buyers.

kinds of agents. Nevertheless, GD agents cannot guarantee to be adaptive to the changes of supply and demand relationships and the dynamic joining or leaving of agents. A-FL agents can work well in some situations, especially when it is hard for the agent to trade. However, there are many parameters to be adjusted with the market fluctuation, which prevents the agents from being adaptive to the dynamic environments from time to time.

Experiments to compare all kinds of agents

Based on the above experiments to compare two kinds of agents in each experiment, it is observed that the performance of AA agents is superior when compared with any other kind of agents. Thus we decided to design the experiments in the following in order to compare all kinds of agents together in one experiment. The main difference is that in the following experiments, at the beginning of each run out of 1000 runs, all the sellers or buyers are randomly selected, while in the above experiments, there are two kinds of sellers or buyers fixed and only the rest of the sellers or buyers are randomly selected.

The experimental setup is that all 100 sellers are selected randomly in each run from a pool that consists of 140 sellers. In this pool, there are 20 AA, 20 ZI-U, 20 ZI-C, 20 ZIP, 20 GD, 20 CP, and 20 A-FL sellers, each of which has one unit of goods to sell. Consequently, the combination of sellers changes in every run. This can simulate that all sellers are free to join or leave the market as they want. All sellers have the same probability of being selected from the pool. Therefore, in 1000 runs, all kinds of sellers in comparison should have almost the same number of submission opportunities for all the units of goods to be traded. The buyers are all ZI-C buyers in order to be fair to different kinds of sellers. To simulate different supply and demand relationships, the number of ZI-C buyers changes from 50, 60, 70, 80, 90, 100, 120, 140, 160, 180, to 200 every 1000 runs. The experimental setup of buyers is similar to that of sellers.

Figures 3.15 and 3.16 clearly show that AA agents behave the best in the dynamic CDA markets under different supply and demand relationships. This result demonstrates again that AA agents are adaptive to dynamic market environments. In addition, ZIP and GD agents gain a lot of profit in these figures, which conforms to the experimental results in Figures 3.9, 3.10, 3.11, 3.12, 3.13, and 3.14. In such a dynamic CDA market, ZIP and GD agents take into account many factors of the market and benefit from their adaptivity to the environment.

3.4 Summary

In this chapter, a new bidding strategy, called AA strategy, has been developed to guide an agent's buying or selling behaviour in a series of CDAs. AA strategy uses heuristic rules and a reasoning mechanism based on two-level adaptive attitudes and an α-ω method to decide what bids or asks to place and to accept. In the two-

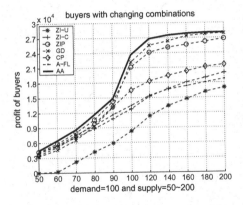
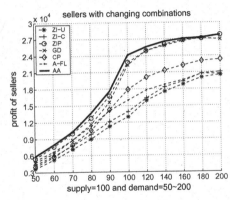

Figure 3.15: Performance of different kinds of buyers in dynamic CDA markets.

Figure 3.16: Performance of different kinds of sellers in dynamic CDA markets.

level adaptive attitudes, eagerness is defined based on the short-term attitude and the long-term attitude, which reflects the realtime supply and demand relation from an agent's point of view. The α-ω method is integrated within the heuristic rules, which tells an agent what kind of asks or bids should be accepted or declined directly in the current market environment.

We benchmark the performance of AA strategy against six conventional alternatives in the literature. The experiments are composed of two groups, experiments to simulate static CDA markets, and experiments to simulate dynamic CDA markets. The experimental results of the first group show the superior performance of AA strategy in static market environments. Supported by the success in static markets, we carry out the second group of experiments to let AA agents compete with other kinds of agents one by one in dynamic market environments. The results also illustrate that AA strategy can outperform any other strategy. Finally, all the bidding strategies are put together in one dynamic CDA market to compete, which again illustrates that AA strategy is the best. These results also demonstrate the importance of eagerness based on two-level adaptive attitudes and the α-ω method with heuristic rules. We view these as our main contribution. We also notice that in some cases, the performance of ZIP, A-FL, or GD agents is quite good compared with that of AA agents. The reason is that ZIP, A-FL, or GD agents can make use of different factors in the market and as a result behave adaptively to the dynamic market.

Chapter 4

Soft Asks and Soft Bids

There are several bidding strategies proposed in the literature for agents in CDAs. For most bidding strategies, the asks or bids determined are hard and cannot be compromised. However, for human traders, we notice that the decisions are usually soft and adaptive in different situations. Therefore, we believe that integrating softness and adaptivity into the bidding strategies can enhance the performance of agents. In this chapter, soft asks and soft bids are defined. Experimental results confirm that when agents using different bidding strategies make soft compromise in various situations, their performance is improved significantly in general. Eagerness is extended on the basis of eagerness in Chapter 3. Fuzzy sets and fuzzy logic rules are employed to decide the value of eagerness in order to cope with uncertainty in the dynamic market. To guide agents to adopt soft asks or bids in dynamic and unknown markets, an adaptive mechanism is proposed to adjust the degree of softness of soft asks or bids according to eagerness. Experimental results show that agents adopting the adaptive mechanism generally outperform the corresponding agents without the adaptive mechanism.

The roadmap of this chapter is organized as follows. Section 4.1 introduces the motivation of soft asks and soft bids. The definitions are given in Section 4.2. In Section 4.3, experiments are designed and implemented to explore the rules on how to adjust the degree of softness with dynamic CDA market. Some observations are described in Section 4.4. Section 4.5 extends eagerness based on the previous version in Chapter 3 and proposes an adaptive mechanism. Section 4.6 presents experimental results of agents utilizing the adaptive mechanism. Section 4.7 concludes this chapter.

Part of the material presented in this chapter has been published in [68].

4.1   Motivation

Consider a human buyer who wants to buy a unit of goods in a CDA market. After taking into account a number of factors, he determines that he should submit a bid about \$100 to buy a unit of goods. If the current *oa* is \$101, then it is possible that the human buyer considers \$101 to be still a good price. It is possible that he accepts the *oa* and buys the unit of goods at \$101. Thus, the decision on whether to accept the current *oa* is not hard. We call the decision soft bid determination.

Of course, if the current *oa* is \$135, then the human buyer might not be willing to transact at \$135 if he finds that he has been able recently to smoothly buy many units of goods. However, the human buyer might be willing to accept \$135 if he feels that it is difficult for him to buy one unit of goods. Therefore, the decision on whether to accept the current *oa* is not only soft, but also adaptive depending on the current market environment, for example, whether it is difficult or easy for the trader to have transactions in the market, and so on. We call such soft decision, adaptive soft bid determination. These decisions often increase transaction opportunities of the trader at good, though not "ideal" prices, and have positive effects on the amount of total profit the trader gains in general.

A characteristic that is common to almost all the previously proposed strategies is that the agent considers all the factors as required by the strategy in use, and computes the ask or bid to be submitted, which is final and hard. A-FL strategy [53] is the only exception with which agents are able to make a fixed soft bid determination. However, the fixed soft bid determination is not adaptive, which means that agents using A-FL strategy do not adjust the degree of softness of the asks or bids according to the changing market. In practical CDA markets, sellers and buyers often enter or depart the market freely; the composition of sellers or buyers is not always the same; one specific degree of softness that is suitable for agents using one kind of bidding strategies under one static market may not work well for agents using other kinds of bidding strategies under different markets. Therefore a fixed soft bid determination is not enough to handle a changing market. We believe that when agents utilize the bidding strategy which integrates the adaptive soft bid determination, their performance can be enhanced in general. The effect of adaptive soft bid determination to agents utilizing different kinds of bidding strategies is investigated in this chapter.

4.2   Definitions

For a seller i, suppose the ask determined by seller i is denoted as $[ask - \delta_s, ask]$, which means that if the current *ob* is higher than or equal to $ask - \delta_s$, a transaction is made at the value of the *ob* and the current round will be ended. Otherwise, the seller will submit *ask* to the market. This kind of asks is called *soft asks* for sellers. δ_s is called the *degree of softness for soft asks* .

Definition 4.2.1. For a seller, a *soft ask* is a tuple (a, δ_s) such that

- if $ob > a - \delta_s$ then the seller accepts ob;

- otherwise, the seller submits a as his ask.

After considering all the factors required by the bidding strategy in use, a buyer j decides to accept any oa which is lower than or equal to $bid + \delta_b$. If there is no acceptable oa, the buyer will submit bid to the market. This kind of bid is called a *soft bid* for buyers. δ_b is called the *degree of softness for soft bids*.

Definition 4.2.2. For a buyer, a *soft bid* is a tuple (b, δ_b) such that

- if $oa < b + \delta_b$ then the buyer accepts oa;

- otherwise, the buyer submits b as his bid.

4.3 Experimental Results and Analysis

Based on the definition of soft asks and soft bids, the key questions are when the adoption of soft asks or bids can enhance profits and what degree of softness should be adopted under different situations. The answer in conjecture is as follows. For an agent, if the current market favors the agent, it is easy for him to make transactions and he should not adopt soft asks or bids. If the current market goes against the agent, it is difficult for him to make transactions and he should adopt soft asks or bids. The degree of softness of soft asks or bids should be increased when it becomes more and more difficult for the agent to make transactions. The experimental results below have demonstrated the relationship between the degree of softness and the situation whether it is easy or difficult for the agent to make transactions

A series of five groups of experiments were conducted corresponding to five kinds of agents utilizing ZI-C, ZIP, CP, GD, and A-FL. For each kind of agents, there are two experiments for sellers and buyers individually. In each experiment, seven sessions are provided in which the supply (demand) changes from 10 to 50 while the demand (supply) is 30. In each session, the profits of two kinds of agents are compared. One is the agents utilizing the bidding strategy X, where X can be ZI-C, ZIP, GD, CP, or A-FL. The other is the agents which employ X adopting soft asks (soft bids), denoted as X_{δ_s} (X_{δ_b}). For the agents utilizing X_{δ_s} (X_{δ_b}), the value of δ_s (δ_b) is changed from $0 \times step$ to $80 \times step$, where $step$ is a small value. In each session, there are 1,000 runs for each specific δ_s (δ_b). In order to compare the profits, the agents utilizing X_{δ_s} (X_{δ_b}) and the agents utilizing X have the same number of units of goods and the same distribution of reservation prices. Besides these two kinds of sellers (buyers), other sellers (buyers) utilize bidding strategies randomly selected from the other four strategies. All the buyers (sellers) utilize ZI-C strategy in order to be fair for all kinds of agents.

4.3.1   Experimental Results for Markets Favoring Agents

Figure 4.1 and Figure 4.2 show that when supply (demand) is 30, 40, and 50 while demand (supply) is 30, buyers (sellers) can trade all their units of goods. The profit of agents utilizing X_{δ_b} (X_{δ_s}) is lower than that of agents utilizing X, where X can be ZI-C, ZIP, CP, GD, and A-FL. The result demonstrates that when the supply (demand) is larger than or equal to the demand (supply), the buyer (seller) agent can smoothly trade all his units of goods and the adoption of soft bids (asks) cannot benefit the buyer (seller) agent. The reasons are as follows. The total number of transactions achieved by the agents utilizing X_{δ_b} (X_{δ_s}) is the same as that of the agents using X; however the average transaction price of the agents using X_{δ_b} (X_{δ_s}) is higher (lower) than that of the agents using X, shown in Figures 4.6(e), 4.6(f), 4.6(g) (Figures 4.4(e), 4.4(f), 4.4(g)). As a result, the profit of agents utilizing X_{δ_b} (X_{δ_s}) is lower than that of agents utilizing X.

4.3.2   Experimental Results for Markets Going Against Agents

Figure 4.1 shows that when the supply (demand) is 10, 15, 20, and 25, the profit of agents using X_{δ_b} (X_{δ_s}) is significantly better than that of agents using X. X in Figure 4.1 can be ZI-C, CP, and GD. In Figure 4.2, when the supply (demand) is 10, 15, and 20, the profit of the agents using ZIP_{δ_b} (ZIP_{δ_s}) is slightly better than or similar to that of ZIP buyers (sellers). When the supply (demand) is 25, the profit of the agents using ZIP_{δ_b} (ZIP_{δ_s}) is less than that of ZIP buyers (sellers). Similar results are shown for agents using $A\text{-}FL_{\delta_b}$ ($A\text{-}FL_{\delta_s}$). In summary, when the market goes against the agent, the agent cannot trade most of his units of goods and the adoption of soft bids or asks can benefit the agent in general.

It can be observed that the performance of agents using ZI-C, CP, and GD with soft asks or bids is enhanced remarkably while the performance of agents utilizing ZIP and A-FL with soft asks or bids is improved moderately or decreased in some cases, *i.e.*, when supply (demand) is 25. In order to explore the reasons, we list the percentage of increase of the number of transactions, which is computed by the number of transactions of agents using X_{δ_s} (X_{δ_b}) minus that of X agents and then divided by the latter. Figure 4.3 (Figure 4.5) shows the percentage of increase for sellers (buyers). It can be seen that the percentage of increase of the number of transactions achieved by the agents using ZI-C, CP, and GD integrated with soft asks or bids is from 20 percent to 100 percent while the percentage of increase achieved by the agents who utilize ZIP and A-FL adopting soft asks or bids is around 20 percent.

At the same time, we also list the percentage of increase of the average transaction price. The value is calculated by the average transaction price of agents using X_{δ_s} (X_{δ_b}) minus that of X agents and then divided by the latter. In Figure 4.4 and Figure 4.6, it can be observed that the percentages of increase of average transaction price for agents using ZI-C, CP, GD, ZIP, and A-FL adopting soft asks or bids are often similar to each other and within 10 percent. Thus the

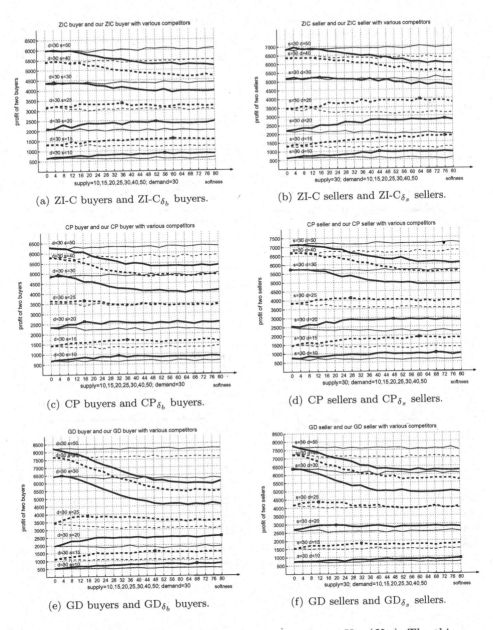

Figure 4.1: The thick curve is the profit of agents using X_{δ_b} (X_{δ_s}). The thin one is the profit of agents using X. In the top three sessions, the profit of X_{δ_b} (X_{δ_s}) agents cannot exceed that of X agents. In the bottom four sessions, the profit of X_{δ_b} (X_{δ_s}) agents is better than that of X agents. X can be ZI-C, CP, and GD in this figure. The square on each curve represents the optimal softness.

significance of the increase in number of transactions achieved by the agents using ZI-C, CP, and GD adopting soft asks or bids explains why their profits are enhanced remarkably.

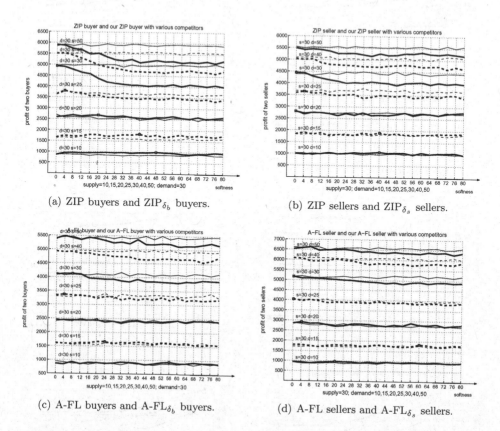

(a) ZIP buyers and ZIP$_{\delta_b}$ buyers.   (b) ZIP sellers and ZIP$_{\delta_s}$ sellers.

(c) A-FL buyers and A-FL$_{\delta_b}$ buyers.   (d) A-FL sellers and A-FL$_{\delta_s}$ sellers.

Figure 4.2: The thick curve is the profit of agents using X_{δ_b} (X_{δ_s}). The thin one is the profit of agents using X. In the top four sessions, the profit of X_{δ_b} (X_{δ_s}) agents cannot exceed that of X agents. In the bottom three sessions, the profit of X_{δ_b} (X_{δ_s}) agents is slightly better than or similar to that of X agents. X can be ZIP and A-FL in this figure. The square on each curve represents the optimal softness.

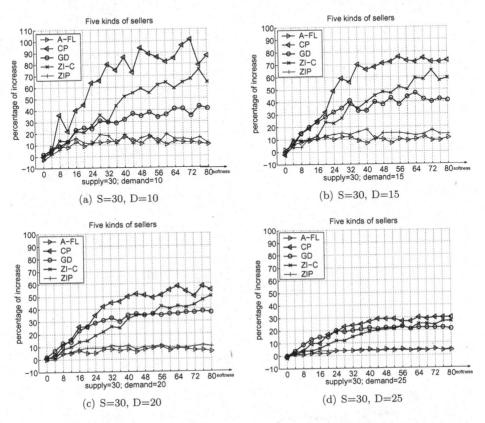

Figure 4.3: The percentage of increase of the number of transactions is calculated by the number of transactions achieved by X_{δ_s} agents minus that of X agents and then divided by the latter. The four figures give four different supply and demand relationships. In each figure, different degrees of softness are included. X can be ZI-C, ZIP, GD, CP, and A-FL in this figure.

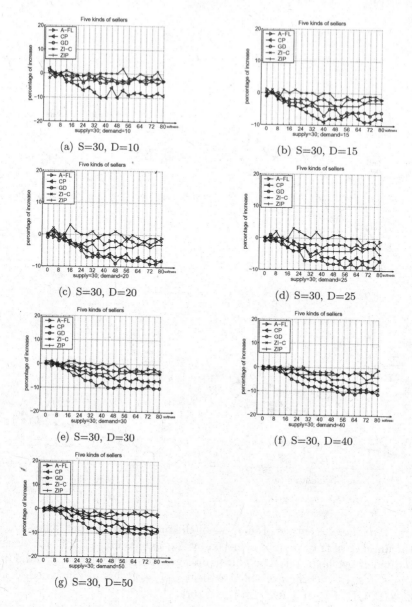

(a) S=30, D=10 (b) S=30, D=15

(c) S=30, D=20 (d) S=30, D=25

(e) S=30, D=30 (f) S=30, D=40

(g) S=30, D=50

Figure 4.4: The percentage of increase of the average transaction price is calculated by the average transaction price achieved by X_{δ_s} agents minus that of X agents and then divided by the latter. The seven figures show seven different supply and demand relationships. In each figure, different degrees of softness are included. X can be ZI-C, ZIP, GD, CP, and A-FL in this figure.

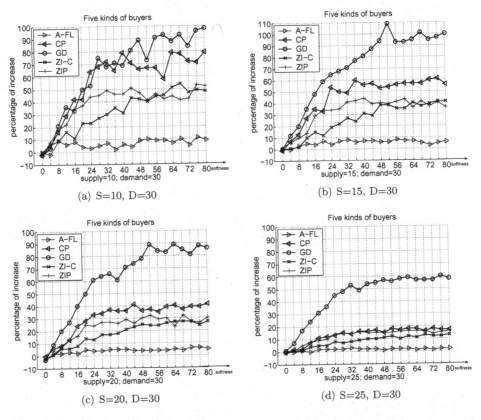

Figure 4.5: The percentage of increase of the number of transactions is calculated by the number of transactions achieved by X_{δ_b} agents minus that of X agents and then divided by the latter. The four figures give four different supply and demand relationships. In each figure, different degrees of softness are included. X can be ZI-C, ZIP, GD, CP, and A-FL in this figure.

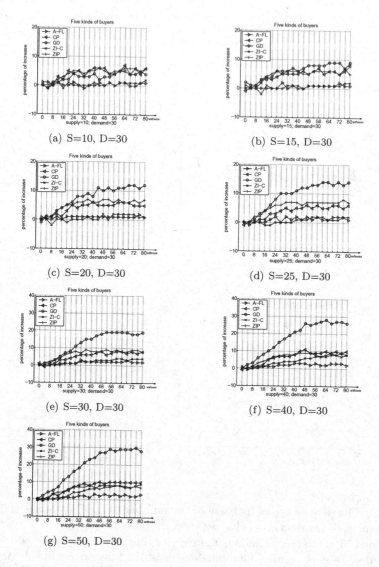

Figure 4.6: The percentage of increase of the average transaction price is calculated by the average transaction price achieved by X_{δ_b} agents minus that of X agents and then divided by the latter. The seven figures show seven different supply and demand relationships. In each figure, different degrees of softness are included. X can be ZI-C, ZIP, GD, CP, and A-FL in this figure.

4.4 Observations

Suppose there are two groups of sellers, group 1 and group 2, among many sellers and many buyers in one CDA market. The sellers in both groups employ the same bidding strategy and have the same distribution of reservation prices and the same number of units of goods. The only difference between these two groups of sellers is that the sellers in group 1 adopt soft asks while the sellers in group 2 do not.

If a transaction is made by a seller who does not adopt soft asks, then when the seller adopts soft asks, such a transaction can also be achieved. If there is no transaction for a seller without adopting soft asks, then when the seller adopts soft asks, there may be a transaction because the seller now is willing to make a compromise with the buyer. A similar conclusion can be achieved for buyers. The corresponding observations are given below.

Observation 1 Consider two groups of sellers in one CDA market. The only difference between these two groups of sellers is that one adopts soft asks while the other does not. The group of sellers who adopt soft asks will in general gain a larger number of transactions than that achieved by the other group of sellers who do not adopt soft asks.

Observation 2 Consider two groups of buyers in one CDA market. The only difference between these two groups of buyers is that one adopts soft bids while the other does not. The group of buyers who adopt soft bids will in general gain a larger number of transactions than that achieved by the other group of buyers who do not adopt soft bids.

From the experimental results shown in Figure 4.3 and Figure 4.5, it can be seen that when the degree of softness is greater than 0, the percentage of increase of the number of transactions achieved by the agents employing ZI-C, CP, GD, ZIP, and A-FL integrated with soft asks or bids are in general significant. The experimental results confirm Observation 1 and Observation 2.

Based on the experimental results in Figure 4.4, a phenomenon is illustrated and described in the following. In one CDA market there are two groups of sellers. The only difference between these two groups of sellers is that one group adopts soft asks while the other does not. The average transaction price of the group of sellers who adopt soft asks will be generally lower than that achieved by another group of sellers who do not adopt soft asks. A similar phenomenon is shown in Figure 4.6, that the average transaction price of the group of buyers who adopt soft bids will be higher than that achieved by the other group of buyers who do not adopt soft bids in general.

In summary, these experiments clearly show the following results:

(1) When the agent can trade all his units of goods, the adoption of soft asks or bids cannot benefit him. Actually, it will decrease the profit of the agent. This can be observed in Figure 4.1 and Figure 4.2. When supply is larger than or equal to demand, all the buyer agents can buy all the units of goods that they desire to buy. The buyer agents with soft bids cannot outperform the buyer agents without soft bids. Similarly, seller agents can reach the same conclusion.

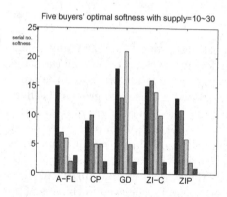

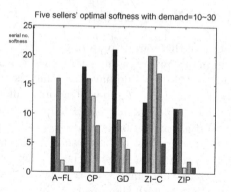

Figure 4.7: Optimal softness of different X_{δ_b} buyers. In each group, the demand is fixed as 30. The supply is changed from 10 to 30 from left to right within a group. The buyers are utilizing A-FL, CP, GD, ZI-C, and ZIP from the left group to the right group.

Figure 4.8: Optimal softness of different X_{δ_s} sellers. In each group, the supply is fixed as 30. The demand is changed from 10 to 30 from left to right within a group. The sellers are utilizing A-FL, CP, GD, ZI-C, and ZIP from the left group to the right group.

(2) When agents cannot trade all units of goods, the adoption of soft asks or bids can enhance the performance of the agents in general. For agents utilizing ZI-C, CP, and GD with soft asks or bids, the performance is enhanced greatly. For ZIP and A-FL agents adopting soft asks or bids, the performance can only be improved moderately or decreased in some cases. The root cause is that the number of transactions achieved by agents using ZI-C, CP, and GD with soft asks or bids exceeds that of ZI-C, CP, and GD agents greatly, while the number of transactions achieved by agents using ZIP and A-FL with soft asks or bids cannot.

(3) Figure 4.7 and Figure 4.8 show that for A-FL, CP, GD, ZI-C, and ZIP agents adopting soft asks or bids, when the supply (demand) changes from 10 to 30 while the demand (supply) remains 30, the general trend of the optimal softness corresponding to the highest profit of the agents is that the degree of softness decreases gradually when the supply (demand) approaches the fixed demand (supply) step by step. Therefore when the agent finds it is difficult to trade all his units of goods, he should increase the value of δ_b (δ_s); otherwise, he should decrease the value of δ_b (δ_s).

In practice, it is hard for one agent to know clearly the realtime supply and demand in a dynamic and unknown CDA market. Therefore, we utilize eagerness to enable an agent to detect the current market environment from his own point of view. When the value of eagerness approaches 1.0, the agent knows that it has been easy for him to have many transactions recently; he should be eager for more profit in the current round; and the degree of softness should be decreased. On the contrary, when the value of eagerness is close to 0, the agent learns that he has difficulty in trading the goods; he should be eager for more transactions in the current round; and the degree of softness should be increased to help him gain more transactions. On the basis of eagerness, the agent has the ability to adapt the degree of softness according to market context. In addition, an adaptive mechanism is proposed to integrate eagerness and softness together with different bidding strategies. Experiments are carried out to demonstrate the good performance of agents brought by the adaptive mechanism.

4.5 Agents with Adaptive Soft Asks or Bids

Eagerness defined in Section 3.1.2 is an indicator of the current supply and demand relationship from an agent's point of view. In this section we extend eagerness by employing a fuzzy set and fuzzy logic-based approach to compute the value of eagerness. Based on eagerness, we provide an adaptive mechanism for agents to adopt soft asks or bids and adjust the degree of softness adaptively.

4.5.1 Eagerness

In Section 3.1.2, eagerness has been defined and denoted as F_{eager}, which is used to represent the degree to which an agent is eager for more transactions or more profits. Two definitions have been introduced to calculate the value of the long-term attitude, $T_{p,i}$, and the short-term attitude, T_i^r.

However, from Definition 3.1.1, it can be seen that the levels of eagerness for different agents cannot be the same even if the value of T_i^r is the same. For example, assume there are two sellers among many sellers in the CDA market, seller1 and seller2. Seller1 has two units of goods to sell and seller2 has ten units of goods to sell. If the current values of T_i^r for two sellers are both 0.1 in the past 10 consecutive rounds, it means that they both have traded 1 unit of goods in the past 10 rounds. However, 1 unit of goods for seller1 is 50 percent of all his units of goods while for seller2 only 10 percent of all his units of goods. Therefore, these two sellers should have different values of eagerness. In order to make the value of T_i^r comparable among all agents, we normalize the value of T_i^r and define the *desired transaction rate* $T_{i,\text{desired}}^r$ and the *normalized transaction rate* $T_{i,\text{normalized}}^r$ as follows.

Definition 4.5.1. Let $NUNIT_{owned}$ be the total number of units agent i wanted to trade in the last run. NUM_{run} is the total number of successful transactions in the last run. The desired transaction rate $T_{i,\text{desired}}^r$ is calculated by:

$$T_{i,\text{desired}}^r = NUNIT_{owned} \div NUM_{run}.$$

1: [rule1] IF $T^r_{i,\text{normalized}}$ is small and $T_{p,i}$ is small   THEN F_{eager} is $\min(T^r_{i,\text{normalized}}, T_{p,i})$;

2: [rule2] IF $T^r_{i,\text{normalized}}$ is small and $T_{p,i}$ is medium   THEN F_{eager} is $\min(T^r_{i,\text{normalized}}, T_{p,i})$;

3: [rule3] IF $T^r_{i,\text{normalized}}$ is small and $T_{p,i}$ is large   THEN F_{eager} is $\min(T^r_{i,\text{normalized}}, T_{p,i}) - \theta$;

4: [rule4] IF $T^r_{i,\text{normalized}}$ is medium and $T_{p,i}$ is small   THEN F_{eager} is $\min(T^r_{i,\text{normalized}}, T_{p,i}) + \theta$;

5: [rule5] IF $T^r_{i,\text{normalized}}$ is medium and $T_{p,i}$ is medium THEN F_{eager} is $\min(T^r_{i,\text{normalized}}, T_{p,i})$;

6: [rule6] IF $T^r_{i,\text{normalized}}$ is medium and $T_{p,i}$ is large   THEN F_{eager} is $\min(T^r_{i,\text{normalized}}, T_{p,i}) - \theta$;

7: [rule7] IF $T^r_{i,\text{normalized}}$ is large and $T_{p,i}$ is small   THEN F_{eager} is $\max(T^r_{i,\text{normalized}}, T_{p,i}) + \theta$;

8: [rule8] IF $T^r_{i,\text{normalized}}$ is large and $T_{p,i}$ is medium   THEN F_{eager} is $\max(T^r_{i,\text{normalized}}, T_{p,i})$;

9: [rule9] IF $T^r_{i,\text{normalized}}$ is large and $T_{p,i}$ is large   THEN F_{eager} is $\max(T^r_{i,\text{normalized}}, T_{p,i})$;

Figure 4.9: The fuzzy rule base for eagerness.

Definition 4.5.2. The normalized transaction rate $T^r_{i,\text{normalized}}$ is calculated by:

$$
T^r_{i,\text{normalized}} = \begin{cases}
T^r_i \div T^r_{i,\text{desired}} & T^r_i \leq T^r_{i,\text{desired}} \text{ and } T^r_{i,\text{desired}} > 0 \\
T^r_i & T^r_{i,\text{desired}} = 0 \\
1 & \text{otherwise}
\end{cases}.
$$

We employ the previous example to explain the meaning of $T^r_{i,\text{normalized}}$. Suppose there are 20 transactions in the last run. Thus the desired transaction rate $T^r_{i,\text{desired}}$ for seller1 is 0.1 and that of seller2 is 0.5. After normalization, the value of $T^r_{i,\text{normalized}}$ for seller1 is 1.0 and that of seller2 is 0.2. There exists a big difference between seller1 and seller2. Consequently, seller2 will be much more eager for transactions compared with seller1.

, The CDA market is dynamic and partially unknown to agents. In addition, information collected from the market is uncertain and imprecise. These reasons lead us to employ fuzzy sets and fuzzy logic [133] in making decisions. We note that there are a huge amount of successful applications based on fuzzy logic and fuzzy control [34], [131], [53]. Among many kinds of fuzzy controllers, Sugeno controller [105] [134] has been widely used in many areas, including the application in [53]. The idea of Sugeno controller is to produce rules of the form:

IF x_1 is A_i and x_2 is A_{i+1} THEN μ_i is $f_i(x_1, x_2)$,

where $i \in [1, n]$, which have fuzzy antecedents and consequences that are func-

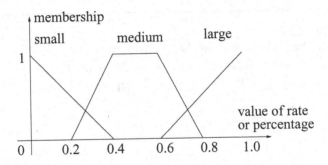

Figure 4.10: The three fuzzy sets used in the reasoning.

tions of the input variables. The output of these rule results is aggregated as weighted sums of each result generated by each rule, denoted as $\mu = (\sum_{i=1}^{n} (\alpha_i \times f_i(x_1, x_2))) / (\sum_{i=1}^{n} \alpha_i)$. α_i is the degree of membership of the input value in the rule antecedent and calculated by: $\alpha_i = \min\{A_i(x_1), A_{i+1}(x_2)\}$.

As required by the Sugeno controller, we define three fuzzy sets, small, medium, and large (shown in Figure 4.10) and provide a set of fuzzy rules (shown in Figure 4.9). The value of *eagerness* is computed by the Sugeno controller based on these fuzzy sets and reasoning rules. The value of eagerness represents the feeling of an agent in a series of CDAs. For any agent, when he could only trade a few units of goods in the past several rounds and he could not trade all his units of goods in the previous run, he will become eager for more transactions. The value of eagerness is small. Thus the agent will submit low asks or high bids in the current round in return for more transactions. On the contrary, if the agent could trade many units of goods in the past several rounds and he could trade all his units of goods in the previous run, he will become eager for more profit. The value of eagerness is large. Therefore the agent will submit high asks or low bids in the current round in order to gain more profits.

4.5.2 Enhancing Bidding Strategies for Sellers and Buyers by Adaptive Soft Asks and Soft Bids

Algorithms have been designed for seller agents and buyer agents utilizing different bidding strategies to integrate the adaptive mechanism. X represents any bidding strategy without integrating the adaptive mechanism. X_{δ_s} (X_{δ_b}) denotes the enhanced bidding strategy for sellers (buyers) with the adaptive mechanism.

The algorithm for sellers is given in Figure 4.11. The enhanced bidding strategy works in the following way. A seller first calculates eagerness, and then computes the degree of softness δ_s according to eagerness, the reservation price, and the highest price of the market. If ob is higher than the value of $ask - \delta_s$, ob is accepted by the seller and a transaction occurs. Otherwise, the seller will submit an ask that is equal to the ask calculated by using strategy X. For buyers, the

1: calculate $F_{eager}^{(i)}$;
2: let $P_{ul}^{(i)}$ be the highest price of the market;
3: let $C_k^{(i)}$ be the reservation price of the current unit of goods;
4: let $\delta_s^{(i)}$ represent the degree of softness of seller i;
5: $\delta_s^{(i)} = (1 - F_{eager}^{(i)}) \times (P_{ul}^{(i)} - C_k^{(i)})$;
6: calculate an *ask* utilizing strategy X;
7: **if** $(ask - \delta_s^{(i)}) < ob$ **then**
8:     accept *ob*; the current round is ended;
9: **else**
10:     submit the *ask*;
11: **end if**

Figure 4.11: The pseudo code of any bidding strategy X with the adaptive mechanism for sellers.

enhanced bidding strategy is shown in Figure 4.12. Similarly, a buyer calculates the value of eagerness and δ_b of soft bids accordingly. If *oa* is lower than $bid + \delta_b$, there is a transaction. Otherwise, the buyer will submit a bid that is equal to the bid calculated by X.

For example, consider a seller. The long-term attitude $T_{p,i}$ is 0.9 and the short-term attitude $T_{i,\text{normalized}}^r$ is 0.3. Then the value of eagerness is 0.29 where θ is 0.01. Suppose the value of $P_{ul}^{(i)}$ is 3.4 and the value of $C_k^{(i)}$ is 1.2. As a result, the degree of softness δ_s of the soft asks is 1.56. It means that when *ob* is larger than $ask - 1.56$, the seller will accept the *ob*. This will be sure to help him grab more transactions. The result also conforms to the intuition of humans. When the seller cannot trade many units of his goods, then he will be more eager to trade his goods in the current round. Consequently, the seller is willing to accept more bids even if the bids are not so profitable. Thus the value of δ_s of soft asks is large.

4.6   Experimental Evaluation

4.6.1   Experimental Setup

This section evaluates the adaptive mechanism by comparing the profit gained by agents using strategy X with the profit achieved by agents using X_{δ_s} (X_{δ_b}) in a variety of dynamic environments, where X_{δ_s} (X_{δ_b}) is X integrated with the adaptive mechanism. X can be ZI-C, ZIP, CP, GD, and A-FL, which represent the most widely cited strategies for agents participating in CDAs. The dynamic environment is characterized by: (1) the relationship of supply and demand is changing every 1000 runs; (2) the combination of agents always changes in every run, which means that participants do not necessarily have similar behaviours in any two successive runs of CDAs.

1: calculate $F_{eager}^{(j)}$;
2: let $P_{ll}^{(j)}$ be the lowest price of the market;
3: let $R_k^{(j)}$ be the reservation price of the current unit of goods;
4: let $\delta_b^{(j)}$ the degree of softness of buyer j;
5: $\delta_b^{(j)} = (1 - F_{eager}^{(j)}) \times (R_k^{(j)} - P_{ll}^{(j)})$;
6: calculate a *bid* utilizing strategy X;
7: **if** $(bid + \delta_b^{(j)}) > oa$ **then**
8:     accept oa; the current round is ended;
9: **else**
10:     submit the *bid*;
11: **end if**

Figure 4.12: The pseudo code of any bidding strategy X with the adaptive mechanism for buyers.

In each run, a seller is endowed with a number of units of goods whose reservation prices are independently drawn from a uniform distribution within $[1.1, 1.3]$. Similarly, the reservation prices for the units of goods needed by a buyer are independently drawn from $[3.1, 3.3]$. As in Section 3.3.1, an agent has a period of thinking time to elapse before submitting an ask or a bid. In order to measure how well an agent performs in a CDA, we evaluate the profit. For a seller i, the total profit on all s units sold in a run is $\sum_{k=1}^{s}(P_k^{(i)} - C_k^{(i)})$ where $P_k^{(i)}$ is the transaction price. Similarly for a buyer j, the total profit on all t units bought in a run is $\sum_{k=1}^{t}(R_k^{(j)} - P_k^{(j)})$. An agent's profit is calculated as the sum of the total profits in 1,000 runs.

The experiments are divided into two parts. The first part is designed for testing five pairs of sellers, *i.e.*, ZI-C and ZI-C$_{\delta_s}$, ZIP and ZIP$_{\delta_s}$, CP and CP$_{\delta_s}$, GD and GD$_{\delta_s}$, A-FL and A-FL$_{\delta_s}$. The second part is designed for five pairs of buyers, *i.e.*, ZI-C and ZI-C$_{\delta_b}$, ZIP and ZIP$_{\delta_b}$, CP and CP$_{\delta_b}$, GD and GD$_{\delta_b}$, A-FL and A-FL$_{\delta_b}$.

In the first part, X is one of ZI-C, ZIP, CP, GD, and A-FL in one experiment. The number of units of goods for X_{δ_s} sellers and that for X sellers are always 5. The reservation prices of all the units of goods to be traded by the sellers utilizing X_{δ_s} are the same as those of X sellers. As to the number of units of goods for the other four kinds of sellers, the initial number for each is 10. In the beginning of each run, we randomly select 20 from 40. Thus the combination of sellers is always changing. The buyers are all ZI-C agents to be fair to different sellers. In any experiment, the demand is changed from 10 to 30 every 1000 runs with the step of 5, while the supply is kept 30. Thus the supply and demand relationship is not static in one experiment. Here we do not include the demand larger than the supply because it has been demonstrated in Section 4.3.1 that when sellers can sell all their units of goods, the adoption of soft asks cannot benefit them. In the second part, the experimental setup of buyers is similar to that of sellers.

4.6.2 Experimental Results

The experiments aim to compare the performance of agents adopting X and X_δ (X_{δ_b} and X_{δ_s}). There are five groups of experimental results for ZI-C, ZIP, CP, GD, and A-FL individually. In each group, there are one for buyers and one for sellers. We divide these five groups into two categories. The first is composed of ZI-C and ZI-C$_\delta$, CP and CP$_\delta$, and GD and GD$_\delta$ (shown in Figure 4.13). The second is composed of ZIP and ZIP$_\delta$, and A-FL and A-FL$_\delta$ agents, shown in Figure 4.14.

Results for GD, ZI-C, and CP agents

Figure 4.13 shows that the profit gained by agents using X_{δ_b} (X_{δ_s}) is significantly better than that of agents using X, where X can be ZI-C, CP, and GD. When the supply is equal to the demand, the profits of X_δ agents and X agents are similar. The reason is that under this situation, all these agents can trade almost all their units of goods, which determines that the eagerness approaches 1 and consequently the degree of softness approaches 0. Therefore the effect of soft asks or bids almost disappears and the profits of X_δ agents and X agents are similar.

Results for ZIP and A-FL agents

It is shown in Figure 4.14 that the profits of ZIP and A-FL agents adopting the adaptive mechanism are slightly better than or similar to that of ZIP and A-FL agents without the adaptive mechanism. In particular, in Figure 4.14(c), the profit of A-FL$_{\delta_b}$ agents is not as good as that of A-FL agents when supply is 20 and demand is 30. The reason is that the percentage of increase of the number of transactions is not big enough, such that the profit of A-FL$_\delta$ agents cannot exceed that of A-FL agents. This phenomenon conforms to the results in Section 4.3.2, which shows the performance of ZIP and A-FL agents can hardly be enhanced by adopting different degrees of softness.

4.6.3 Summary and Discussion

In general, adoption of the adaptive mechanism will benefit agents when they cannot trade all their units of goods, which is shown in Figure 4.13 and Figure 4.14. There are several reasons for good performance of agents with the adaptive mechanism to adjust the degree of softness for soft asks or bids. First, the adaptive mechanism enables one agent to learn the current supply and demand situation from his own point of view, which is a meaningful and practical guidance for the agent to rely on. Second, an agent with the adaptive mechanism can learn to

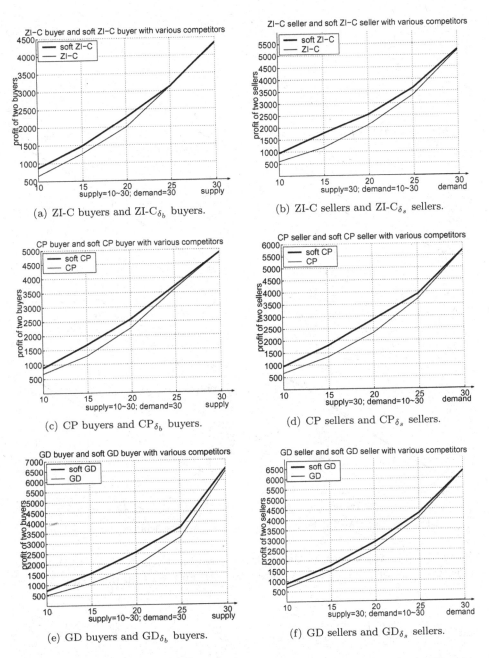

Figure 4.13: The thick curve is the profit of agents utilizing X_{δ_b} (X_{δ_s}). The thin one is the profit of agents using X. X can be ZI-C, CP, and GD in this figure.

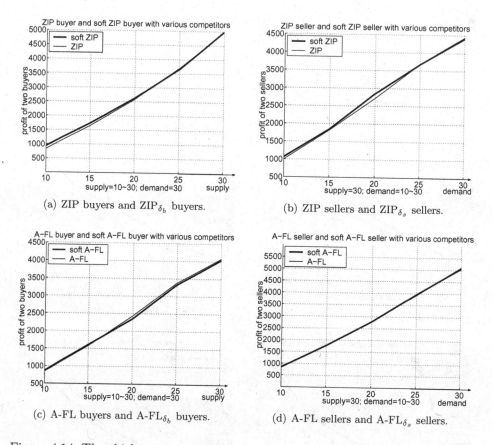

(a) ZIP buyers and ZIP$_{\delta_b}$ buyers.

(b) ZIP sellers and ZIP$_{\delta_s}$ sellers.

(c) A-FL buyers and A-FL$_{\delta_b}$ buyers.

(d) A-FL sellers and A-FL$_{\delta_s}$ sellers.

Figure 4.14: The thick curve is the profit of agents utilizing X_{δ_b} (X_{δ_s}). The thin one is the profit of agents using X. X can be ZIP and A-FL in this figure.

adjust the degree of soft asks or bids, so as to prevent himself from being too soft or too hard. When the agent can trade most of his goods, he will adjust the value of δ (δ_s and δ_b) to be small. Otherwise, he will adjust the value of δ to be large. However, other agents without the adaptive mechanism cannot learn such lessons from experience. Third, in Figure 4.13 and Figure 4.14, it can be seen that the profit of X_δ agents will gradually approach that of X agents. This phenomenon is natural because when the difference between the supply and the demand becomes smaller and smaller, the agents employing strategy X_δ can trade more and more units of goods. Thus the value of δ is smaller and smaller, which causes the effect of soft asks or bids to be weak. Thus the profit of X_δ agents becomes close to that of X agents.

4.7 Summary

This chapter introduces the motivation and the concept of soft asks or bids for agents in CDAs. Experimental results and analysis have illustrated that: (1) when agents can trade all their units of goods, they should not adopt soft asks or bids; (2) when the agents cannot trade all their units of goods, the adoption of soft asks or bids can benefit them; (3) when an agent finds it difficult to make transactions, he should increase the degree of softness; otherwise, he should decrease the degree of softness. In order to guide agents to adopt soft asks or bids in a dynamic CDA market, an adaptive mechanism is presented, which enables agents to make a soft decision according to the current market context. The key component of the adaptive mechanism is eagerness which is extended from the eagerness in Chapter 3 by means of a fuzzy sets and fuzzy logic-based approach. Algorithms for sellers and buyers to integrate the adaptive mechanism are given. Experiments to evaluate agents using ZI-C, ZIP, GD, A-FL, and CP with the adaptive mechanism are also implemented, which demonstrate that in general the adaptive mechanism can remarkably enhance the performance of agents using different bidding strategies in CDAs.

Chapter 5

Adaptive Judgement of Price Acceptability

There are several bidding strategies in the literature for agents in CDAs to employ, any of which can achieve a good performance. Nevertheless, almost none of these strategies judge whether a price is acceptable before the agents calculate their own asks or bids. [53] by He *et al.* is the only work in the literature in which the judgement of price acceptability is incorporated into the bidding strategy. With the judgement of price acceptability, agents can improve their profit by accepting asks or bids directly or submitting no asks or bids until they have computed them.

However, the issues of whether price acceptability can generally improve the performance of agents utilizing different bidding strategies and how to adjust thresholds of price acceptability within dynamic CDA markets, are interesting problems yet to be addressed. Therefore the research discussed in this chapter explores these problems. Experimental results have demonstrated that the judgement of price acceptability can enhance the performance of agents. In order to enable agents to adopt this approach, we propose an adaptive mechanism. The core of the adaptive mechanism is eagerness, which was introduced in Chapter 3 and extended in Chapter 4. Experimental results show that agents adopting the adaptive mechanism remarkably outperform agents without the mechanism.

The remainder of this chapter is organized as follows. Section 5.1 describes the motivation of price acceptability. Section 5.2 defines the judgement of price acceptability. Experiments are designed and conducted in Section 5.3 to detect the general rules of adjusting price acceptability within the market. Section 5.4 proposes the adaptive mechanism of judgement of price acceptability for agents using different bidding strategies in CDAs. Section 5.5 presents experimental results of agents adopting the adaptive mechanism. Section 5.6 concludes this chapter.

Part of the material presented in this chapter has been published in [70].

5.1 Motivation

Suppose a human buyer needs to buy some units of goods in a CDA market. The current oa is $1.5. Based on the trading history of the market, he knows that the oa is profitable enough for him. In addition, suppose he has had few transactions in the past several consecutive rounds. Naturally, he is eager for transactions in the current round. In this case, it is very likely that he will accept the oa, $1.5, immediately. However, if the current ob is $3.0, the human buyer thinks that it is a very high price considering the trading history of the market and his experience. It would be hard for him to submit an even higher bid so as to replace the ob. Therefore the human buyer normally will not be willing to submit any new bid to the current round. We call this kind of behaviour the judgement of price acceptability for buyers.

We notice that for human buyers, the judgement of price acceptability is not static. Instead, it is always changing, conditioning on the market context. Consider the market in the above paragraph. Suppose the human buyer consecutively succeeds in many transactions at the price of about $1.5. Then if the current oa is $1.5, he is not willing to accept the oa. Assume oa is $1.25. If the human buyer thinks it is a profitable price based on his experience and the trading history, he will accept the oa directly. We call this dynamic process the adaptive judgement of price acceptability for buyers. A formal definition of the judgement of price acceptability for buyers is given in the following.

5.2 Definitions

Definition 5.2.1. For a buyer, the *judgement of price acceptability* consists of two thresholds α_b and ω_b such that

- α_b is lower than or equal to ω_b;
- if $oa \leq \alpha_b$, then the buyer accepts oa;
- if $ob \geq \omega_b$, then the buyer submits no bid;
- otherwise, the buyer computes a bid using some strategy X.

Similarly, we can define the judgement of price acceptability for sellers.

Definition 5.2.2. For a seller, the *judgement of price acceptability* consists of two thresholds α_s and ω_s such that

- α_s is lower than or equal to ω_s;
- if $oa \leq \alpha_s$, then the seller submits no ask;
- if $ob \geq \omega_s$, then the seller accepts ob;
- otherwise, the seller computes an ask using some strategy X.

If X denotes any bidding strategy, $X_{\alpha_b}^{\omega_b}$ is defined to represent the strategy X integrated with the judgement of price acceptability for buyers. Similarly, $X_{\alpha_s}^{\omega_s}$ represents X integrated with the judgement of price acceptability for sellers. X_α^ω represents both $X_{\alpha_s}^{\omega_s}$ and $X_{\alpha_b}^{\omega_b}$.

5.3 Experimental Results and Analysis

As to the previous questions on whether the judgement of price acceptability can generally improve the performance of agents using different kinds of strategies and how to adjust the thresholds of price acceptability within dynamic markets, our conjecture is that the judgement of price acceptability can benefit agents under different market situations; when the buyer can trade all the units of goods, the values of α_b and ω_b should be small; otherwise, α_b and ω_b should be large; for seller agents, their profit will be enhanced with large values of α_s and ω_s when easy to sell and with small values of α_s and ω_s when difficult to sell. The following experiments are designed and implemented to test and then confirm the above conjecture.

5.3.1 Experimental Setup

In the experiments, five kinds of bidding strategies are investigated, namely, ZI-C, ZIP, CP, GD, and A-FL, which are the most widely cited bidding strategies in the literature of CDAs. For each kind of strategy X, the effect of the judgement of price acceptability is explored for sellers and buyers respectively by comparing the profit gained by X_α^ω agents and that of X agents. X can be ZI-C, ZIP, CP, GD, or A-FL.

In the experiments for buyers, the demand is fixed as 30 while the supply can be 24, or 30, or 36. Under one specific supply and demand relationship, the value of α_b is selected from the range of $[1.1, 3.3]$ with a step of 0.2. The range of $[1.1, 3.3]$ covers all the feasible asks and bids in the market. In addition, we also include 0 as a value of α_b, which simulates no effect of α_b. For each value of α_b, the value of ω_b is generated from the range of $[\alpha_b, 3.3]$ with a step of 0.2. In addition, we also include a very large value for ω_b to simulate there is no effect of ω_b. For each pair of α_b and ω_b, 1000 runs are carried out.

In order to compare the profit of $X_{\alpha_b}^{\omega_b}$ buyers and that of X buyers, the number of units of goods and the distribution of reservation prices are identical for these two kinds of buyers in each run. The rest of the buyers can randomly select any bidding strategy from ZI-C, ZIP, CP, GD, and A-FL except X and $X_{\alpha_b}^{\omega_b}$, while the demand is always 30. All the sellers are ZI-C sellers in order to be fair to all buyers. The experiment setup for sellers is similar to that for buyers.

5.3.2   Experimental Results and Analysis

Figures 5.1, 5.2, and 5.3 compare the profit of ZI-C$^{\omega_b}_{\alpha_b}$ buyers and that of ZI-C buyers for three different supply and demand relationships. To save space, we extract 4 out of 13 values of α_b, each of which has several correspondent values of ω_b. When the supply is greater than or equal to the demand, the buyers can buy all the units of goods. The profit of $X^{\omega_b}_{\alpha_b}$ buyers is better than that of X buyers especially when the values of α_b and ω_b are small (shown by the solid curve in Figures 5.1(a) and 5.2(a)). The values of α_b and ω_b corresponding to the highest profit are obviously smaller than the average transaction price[1], denoted as $\hat{P}$, of the market in Figures 5.1(a) and 5.2(a). When the supply is smaller than the demand, which means that it is difficult for buyers to trade all, the profit of $X^{\omega_b}_{\alpha_b}$ buyers exceeds that of X buyers especially when the values of α_b and ω_b are large (shown by the solid curve in Figures 5.3(c)). The values of α_b and ω_b of the highest profit are larger than the average transaction price of the market which is shown as a bold vertical line in the figures.

Similarly, the profit of ZI-C sellers can be significantly enhanced by adopting different thresholds of price acceptability, as shown in Figures 5.4, 5.5, and 5.6. It can be observed that when the supply is greater than the demand, sellers have difficulty in trading their goods; the profit of $X^{\omega_s}_{\alpha_s}$ sellers is decreases with a decrease of the values of α_s and ω_s, shown by the solid curves in Figure 5.6. The highest profit for sellers occurs when the values of α_s and ω_s are smaller than $\hat{P}$. On the contrary, when it is easy for sellers to trade their goods, their profit increases with an increase of the values of α_s and ω_s, shown by the solid curves in Figures 5.4 and 5.5. The highest profit for sellers occurs when the values of α_s and ω_s are larger than $\hat{P}$. In [69], the results of the other four kinds of agents are illustrated to be similar to those of ZI-C agents.

In order to clearly show the trend of the optimal values of α_b and ω_b corresponding to the highest profit of ZI-C$^{\omega_b}_{\alpha_b}$ buyers under different supply and demand relationship, we list the optimal values in Figures 5.1, 5.2, and 5.3 in Table 5.1. It can be observed that when the supply is larger than or equal to demand, which means that it is easy for buyers to trade all the units of goods, the values of α_b and ω_b are both smaller than the average transaction price of the market; when the supply is smaller than demand, buyers cannot trade all the goods; in this case, the values of α_b and ω_b are greater than $\hat{P}$; moreover, the larger the supply, the smaller α_b and ω_b. For ZI-C$^{\omega_s}_{\alpha_s}$ sellers (in Figures 5.4, 5.5, and 5.6), the result is similarly shown in Table 5.2. As for the other four kinds of agents, similar results are shown in [69].

Based on the above experiment results, the following conclusions can be made.

- The adoption of certain thresholds of the judgement of price acceptability

---

[1]Generally speaking, the transaction prices in CDA markets often converge to a competitive equilibrium price quickly. Therefore, the transaction prices provide an important point for reference. To reflect this fact, we select the average transaction price as a reference.

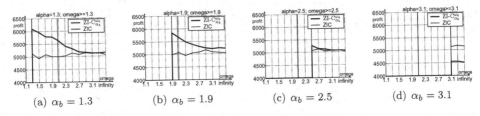

Figure 5.1: ZI-C buyers and ZI-C$^{\omega_b}_{\alpha_b}$ buyers when supply is 36 and demand is 30. The vertical line in the middle of each figure shows the average transaction price.

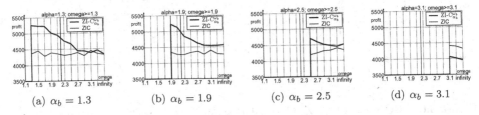

Figure 5.2: ZI-C buyers and ZI-C$^{\omega_b}_{\alpha_b}$ buyers when supply and demand are both 30. The vertical line in the middle of each figure shows the average transaction price.

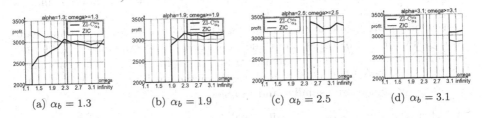

Figure 5.3: ZI-C buyers and ZI-C$^{\omega_b}_{\alpha_b}$ buyers when supply is 24 and demand is 30. The vertical line in the middle of each figure shows the average transaction price.

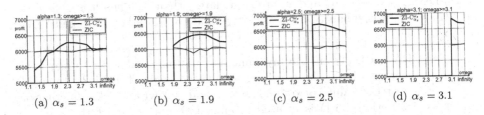

Figure 5.4: ZI-C sellers and ZI-C$^{\omega_s}_{\alpha_s}$ sellers when supply is 30 and demand is 36. The vertical line in the middle of each figure shows the average transaction price.

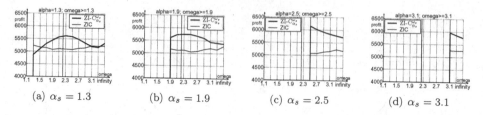

Figure 5.5: ZI-C sellers and ZI-C$^{\omega_s}_{\alpha_s}$ sellers when supply and demand are both 30. The vertical line in the middle of each figure shows the average transaction price.

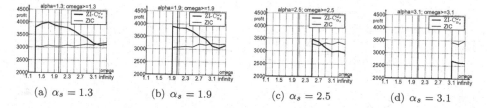

Figure 5.6: ZI-C sellers and ZI-C$^{\omega_s}_{\alpha_s}$ sellers when supply is 30 and demand is 24. The vertical line in the middle of each figure shows the average transaction price.

can significantly improve the performance of agents under different market situations. In detail, if it is easy for a buyer to make many transactions, the values of α_b and ω_b are small. On the contrary, if it is more and more difficult for him to trade, the values of α_b and ω_b become larger and larger. For a seller, if it is easy for him to trade, the values of α_s and ω_s are large. On the contrary, if it is more and more difficult for him to trade, the values of α_s and ω_s become smaller and smaller.

- When the buyer can trade all the units of goods, the profit is enhanced especially when the values of α_b and ω_b are small, smaller than $\hat{P}$. Otherwise, the profit is superior when the values of α_b and ω_b are large, larger than $\hat{P}$. For seller agents, when it is easy to make transactions, good profit occurs when the values of α_s and ω_s are large, larger than $\hat{P}$; when it is difficult to trade, profit is enhanced a lot when the values of α_s and ω_s are smaller than $\hat{P}$.

The CDA market is usually dynamic and partially unknown to agents. It is hard for agents to know the real-time supply and demand. In order to enable agents to adjust the values of α_b and ω_b (α_s and ω_s) with market fluctuation, eagerness (in Section 4.5.1) is utilized to enable agents to detect the real-time market situation. Consider buyer agents. When the value of eagerness is small, the buyer agent knows that it is difficult to buy as many units as he desires. He will increase the values of α_b and ω_b gradually. On the contrary, when the

Table 5.1: The Trend of α_b and ω_b for ZI-C Buyers

Supply	Demand	α_b	ω_b	$\hat{P}$
36	30	1.3	1.3	2.09
30	30	1.5	1.5	2.2
24	30	2.5	2.5	2.37

Table 5.2: The Trend of α_s and ω_s for ZI-C Sellers

Supply	Demand	α_s	ω_s	$\hat{P}$
30	36	3.1	3.1	2.34
30	30	2.5	2.5	2.22
30	24	1.5	1.7	2.04

value of eagerness approaches 1.0, it means that the buyer agent can easily buy all the units he desires. He will decrease the values of α_b and ω_b. For sellers, the adaptive rule is similar to that of buyers. When the value of eagerness is small, the seller should decrease the values of α_s and ω_s gradually. Otherwise, when the value of eagerness is large, the seller should increase the values of α_s and ω_s. As a consequence, an agent can adjust the values of α_b and ω_b (α_s and ω_s) according to eagerness which reveals the current market situation from the agent's own point of view. The adaptive mechanism of the judgement of price acceptability is proposed in the following. Experiments are implemented to demonstrate the significance of the adaptive mechanism to an agent's performance.

5.4 Agents with Adaptive Judgement of Price Acceptability

Now, on the basis of eagerness, we provide an adaptive mechanism of the judgement of price acceptability in a dynamic and unknown CDA market. The adaptive mechanism of judgement of price acceptability for sellers is given in Figure 5.7. A seller first computes the values of α_s and ω_s according to eagerness, the average transaction price, the maximal transaction price, and the minimal transaction price (shown from line 1 to line 10). If the ob is profitable enough, he will accept the ob; if the oa is not big, he will submit no ask; otherwise, he will utilize X to calculate his ask, shown from line 11 to line 16. For buyers, the adaptive mechanism is similar to that of sellers and shown in Figure 5.8.

In the pseudo code, m is a length of rounds to record the transaction prices. If the value of m is too large, the agent will adjust his behaviour in a slow manner that is not sensitive to the dynamic market. A fuzzy set F_{eager} *is close_to 1.0* is employed, which represents the distance from the current value of F_{eager} to 1.0. $dthresh$ is the threshold for the fuzzy set. λ is a pre-specified constant value. If the value of λ is too large, it will weaken the good performance brought by ω. If the value of λ is too small, it will decrease the agent's transaction opportunities.

1: calculate F_{eager};
2: $\hat{P}$=average transaction price in the past m rounds;
3: P_{max}=the maximal transaction price in the past m rounds;
4: P_{min}=the minimal transaction price in the past m rounds;
5: C_{ik} is the reservation price; λ is a pre-specified constant value.
6: **if** (F_{eager} is *close_to* 1.0) **then**
7:     $\omega_s = \hat{P} + (P_{max} - \hat{P}) \times (F_{eager} - dthresh); \alpha_s = \omega_s - \lambda;$
8:     /* when it is easy to sell, ω_s and α_s are larger than $\hat{P}$; the easier, the larger.
       */
9: **else**
10:     $\omega_s = \hat{P} - (\hat{P} - \max(P_{min}, C_{ik})) \times (dthresh - F_{eager}); \alpha_s = \omega_s - \lambda;$
11:     /* when it is difficult to sell, ω_s and α_s are smaller than $\hat{P}$; the more difficult,
        the smaller. */
12: **end if**
13: **if** $ob \geq \omega_s$ **then**
14:     $P_t = ob$; The round is ended;
15: **else if** $oa \leq \alpha_s$ **then**
16:     submit no ask;
17: **else**
18:     calculate an ask utilizing strategy X;
19: **end if**

Figure 5.7: The pseudo code of the adaptive mechanism for seller agents.

1: calculate F_{eager};

2: $\hat{P}$=average transaction price in the past m rounds;

3: P_{max}=the maximal transaction price in the past m rounds;

4: P_{min}=the minimal transaction price in the past m rounds;

5: R_{jk} is the reservation price; λ is a pre-specified constant value.

6: **if** (F_{eager} is *close_to* 1.0) **then**

7: $\quad \alpha_b = \hat{P} - (\hat{P} - P_{min}) \times (F_{eager} - dthresh); \omega_b = \alpha_b + \lambda;$

8: **else**

9: $\quad \alpha_b = \hat{P} + (\max(P_{max}, R_{jk}) - \hat{P}) \times (dthresh - F_{eager}); \omega_b = \alpha_b + \lambda;$

10: **end if**

11: **if** $ob \geq \omega_b$ **then**

12: $\quad$ submit no bid;

13: **else if** $oa \leq \alpha_b$ **then**

14: $\quad P_t = oa$; The round is ended;

15: **else**

16: $\quad$ calculate a bid utilizing strategy X;

17: **end if**

Figure 5.8: The pseudo code of the adaptive mechanism for buyer agents.

5.5 Experimental Evaluation

5.5.1 Experimental Setup

The effect of the adaptive mechanism of judgement of price acceptability is evaluated by comparing the profit of X agents with that of agents using $X_{\alpha_s}^{\omega_s}$ ($X_{\alpha_b}^{\omega_b}$), where X is ZI-C, ZIP, CP, GD, or A-FL strategy. There are experiments for six kinds of sellers, *i.e.*, ZI-C, ZIP, CP, GD, A-FL, and $X_{\alpha_s}^{\omega_s}$ and the experiments for six kinds of buyers, *i.e.*, ZI-C, ZIP, CP, GD, A-FL, and $X_{\alpha_b}^{\omega_b}$. In the experiments for buyers, the number of units of goods of $X_{\alpha_b}^{\omega_b}$ buyers and that of X buyers are both 5. In addition, the distribution of reservation prices of these two kinds of buyers is also the same so that their profit can be compared. As to the number of units of goods for the other four kinds of buyers, the initial number for each is 10. In the beginning of each run, we randomly select 20 units of goods from 40. Thus the combination of buyers is always changing. The sellers are all ZI-C agents in order to be fair to different buyers. In any one experiment, the supply is gradually changed from 15 to 20, 25, 30, 40, 50, and 60 every 1000 runs, while the demand is kept at 30. Thus the supply and demand relationship changes in one experiment. In the experiments for sellers, the setup is similar to that for buyers.

In each run, a seller is endowed with a number of units of goods whose reservation prices are independently drawn from a uniform distribution within $[1.1, 1.3]$. A buyer is endowed with a number of units of goods whose reservation prices are independently drawn from a uniform distribution within $[3.1, 3.3]$. In addition, as in Section 3.3.1, a time lapse occurs during which the agent has time to think before submitting an ask or a bid. We evaluate the performance of an agent by his profit in 1000 runs. For a seller i, the total profit on all s units sold in a run is $\sum_{k=1}^{s}(P_{ik} - C_{ik})$, where P_{ik} is the transaction price. Similarly for a buyer j, the total profit on all t units bought in a run is $\sum_{k=1}^{t}(R_{jk} - P_{jk})$.

The threshold for the fuzzy set, $dthresh$, is 0.8 in the experiments since the value of F_{eager} is between 0.0 and 1.0. λ is set to 0.2 considering the maximal transaction price of the market is about 3.2. m is set to be 30 rounds considering there are altogether 1000 runs.

5.5.2   Experimental Results

From the results shown in Figures 5.9 to 5.18, it can be seen that X_α^ω agents always perform much better than X agents. This demonstrates that the adaptive mechanism does work well. For ZI-C agents, the profit of ZI-C$_\alpha^\omega$ agents is evenly and remarkably better than that of ZI-C agents. For the agents employing GD, ZIP, CP, and A-FL, their profit is not evenly increased under different supply and demand relationships. The reason is that GD, ZIP, CP, and A-FL agents have various levels of learning ability in their bidding strategies.

In Figure 5.16, the profit of GD$_{\alpha_s}^{\omega_s}$ sellers is similar to that of GD sellers when the supply is 30 and the demand is 60. The reasons are as follows. When the demand is much larger than the supply, the profits of all sellers are greatly improved since it is very easy to sell their goods. The profits of GD sellers are the best compared with other kinds of sellers except GD$_{\alpha_s}^{\omega_s}$ sellers. Therefore the room left for GD$_{\alpha_s}^{\omega_s}$ sellers to exceed GD sellers is narrow. As a result, the profits of GD sellers and GD$_{\alpha_s}^{\omega_s}$ sellers are similar. For the case of GD$_{\alpha_b}^{\omega_b}$ buyers, the phenomenon is the same, shown in Figure 5.15.

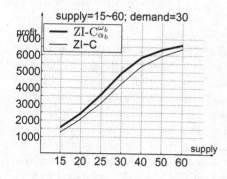
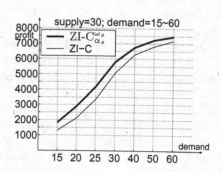

Figure 5.9: ZI-C buyers and ZI-C$_{\alpha_b}^{\omega_b}$ buyers.

Figure 5.10: ZI-C sellers and ZI-C$_{\alpha_s}^{\omega_s}$ sellers.

As can be seen from Figures 5.9 to 5.18, the performance of X agents can be remarkably enhanced by integrating the adaptive mechanism to adjust the thresh-

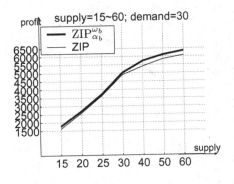

Figure 5.11: ZIP buyers and $\text{ZIP}^{\omega_b}_{\alpha_b}$ buyers.

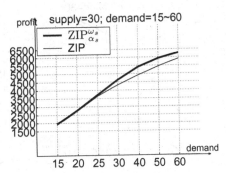

Figure 5.12: ZIP sellers and $\text{ZIP}^{\omega_s}_{\alpha_s}$ sellers.

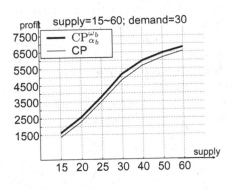

Figure 5.13: CP buyers and $\text{CP}^{\omega_b}_{\alpha_b}$ buyers.

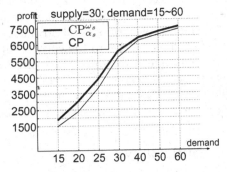

Figure 5.14: CP sellers and $\text{CP}^{\omega_s}_{\alpha_s}$ sellers.

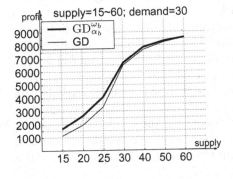

Figure 5.15: GD buyers and $\text{GD}^{\omega_b}_{\alpha_b}$ buyers.

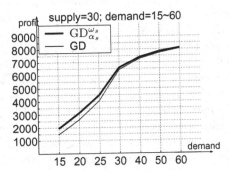

Figure 5.16: GD sellers and $\text{GD}^{\omega_s}_{\alpha_s}$ sellers.

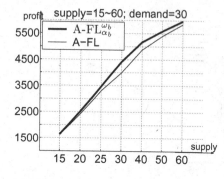

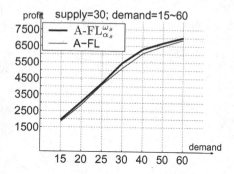

Figure 5.17: A-FL buyers and A-FL$^{\omega_b}_{\alpha_b}$ buyers.

Figure 5.18: A-FL sellers and A-FL$^{\omega_s}_{\alpha_s}$ sellers.

olds of price acceptability under different supply and demand relationships. In contrast to agents without the adaptive mechanism, those who adopt the adaptive mechanism achieve several advantages. First, the agents with the adaptive mechanism are sensitive to the current supply and demand relationship, which is a meaningful guide to adjust their thresholds of price acceptability. Second, the ability to accept asks or bids without hesitation helps the agents grab many profitable transactions. Third, the ability to submit no asks or bids to the market with little profit left protects the agents from being trapped in unprofitable trades.

5.6   Summary

In this chapter, the judgement of price acceptability has been introduced. The effect of the judgement of price acceptability to different kinds of strategies were investigated. Experimental results demonstrate that adoption of the judgement of price acceptability can enhance the performance of agents. When a buyer experiences a change from easy trading of all his goods to difficult trading of some goods, the thresholds of price acceptability will accordingly change from below the average transaction price of the market to above the average transaction price. For a seller, the result is similar. Based on the results, an adaptive mechanism for the judgement of price acceptability is proposed to enable agents to decide whether oa or ob is acceptable or not before they calculate their asks or bids. Experiments on agents utilizing ZI-C, ZIP, GD, A-FL, and CP with the adaptive mechanism are also implemented. Compared with agents without the adaptive mechanism, the performance of agents with the adaptive mechanism is remarkably enhanced in various environments, where both the supply and demand relationship and the combination of agents are constantly changing.

Chapter 6

Adaptive Time Strategies

A market mechanism is a set of rules that governs interactions among buyers and sellers and determines how to form a deal [113]. In many real-world situations it is essential to conclude a negotiation among agents within a fixed deadline. For example, there are continuous double auctions over the Internet that require the trading period to terminate within 24 hours. Recently, auction designers have researched the effect of deadlines in auction mechanisms and have applied them to many electronic commerce applications, such as eBay and Amazon [26].

There are primarily two types of deadlines used in different kinds of auctions. One type is a fixed time for terminating a round of an auction and no extension is allowed. If the pre-specified deadline of a round is reached, all the buyers and sellers have to leave the market no matter whether there is a transaction or not. The other type is *a deadline of inactive interval*, which is a pre-specified interval with no activities since the last valid ask or bid is submitted. With this type of rules, the auction is ended if a sufficiently long interval of time without any updating of outstanding asks or outstanding bids has passed.

To the best of our knowledge, none of the papers in the existing literature on continuous double auctions has given a systematic treatment of incorporating deadlines into the trading process.

For this case, we consider in this chapter continuous double auctions with a fixed deadline. The specific contributions of this chapter are as follows. Firstly, time strategies of agents are defined for buyers and sellers according to which agents can arrange their behaviours. Secondly, the effect of different time strategies on the profit of agents submitting circumstance-dependent soft asks and bids is evaluated by experiments. Through experiments, the following rules are revealed. When an agent finds it easy to trade all his goods, he should wait some time before taking any actions in the market and instead utilize a delayed submission time. Otherwise, when an agent finds it difficult to make transactions, he should try to expedite his thinking as much as possible and adopt an early submission time. A special market situation is detected, which we call "illusory seller's or buyer's market". In detail, for a seller (buyer), when supply is larger (smaller) than demand, it should be more difficult for the seller (buyer) to trade most of his goods; however, the seller (buyer) can indeed trade most of his goods. In order to handle this case, circumstance-dependent negative softness is introduced, which stops the agent from making compromises and increases his profit. Experimental results demonstrate that when encountering an illusory seller's or buyer's market, adopting circumstance-dependent negative softness can enhance the agent's profit in general. Thirdly, based on these results and eagerness in Section 4.5.1, an adaptive mechanism is designed to guide agents employing various bidding strategies to consider the effect of time. Fuzzy concepts [133] are applied in the mechanism. Experimental results demonstrate that agents with the adaptive mechanism perform better than agents without the adaptive mechanism.

The remainder of this chapter is organized as follows. In Section 6.1, the related work is given. Section 6.2 gives the motivation of different time strategies and formal definitions. In Section 6.3, a special market situation, illusory seller's or buyer's market, is detected and analyzed in CDA markets with a fixed deadline. Circumstance dependent soft asks and bids are introduced in Section 6.4. In Section 6.5, rules are provided to adjust submission time according to market situations. An adaptive mechanism is proposed in Section 6.6 and experimental evaluation is given in Section 6.7. Section 6.8 concludes this chapter.

Part of the material presented in this chapter has been published in [71].

6.1 Preliminaries

The definition of continuous double auctions with a fixed deadline was introduced in Section 2.2.2. The main characteristics of this type of CDAs are that the fixed deadline to end each round is pre-specified before executing CDAs; if a transaction occurrs on or before the deadline, the round is terminated; if there is no transaction within the deadline, the round will end at the fixed deadline.

6.1.1 Related Work

In Chapter 4, rules are explored for agents to adopt soft asks and soft bids in dynamic CDA markets. If it is easy for an agent to trade all his goods, he should not make any compromise; otherwise, he should increase the degree of compromise step by step. We call the compromise *softness* of asks or bids. Soft asks and soft bids are defined to be the asks and bids with a range within which an agent can make compromises. An adaptive mechanism is designed to guide agents utilizing different bidding strategies to adopt soft asks and soft bids in a dynamic CDA market. Experimental results show that their profit can be remarkably improved in general by utilizing the adaptive mechanism, called *adaptive bid softness determination*. In this chapter, we denote any bidding strategy X integrated with the adaptive mechanism as X_{Soft}, where X can be ZI-C, ZIP, CP, GD, or A-FL.

None of the previous bidding strategies proposed for CDAs in the literature consider time issues in continuous double auctions. However, time limits or deadlines have been widely explored in many related auction mechanisms. David *et al.* [26] consider a procurement multi-attribute English auction with a deadline. They define a new deadline rule which can diminish the phenomenon of the last-minute bidding strategy and prevent bottlenecks in an agent's network. Choi and Liu [15] propose a new market mechanism for time-constrained trading where agents are associated with a fixed deadline and a search cost. Nevertheless, statistical information about the goods should be provided to buyers and sellers in order to achieve a fair allocation among agents. A one-to-one negotiation model with incomplete information under time constraint is built and analyzed by Cao and Xu [10].

Besides the theoretical analysis of time effect, some researchers are interested in online auctions in real life. For example, auctions on eBay have a fixed end time, while auctions on Amazon are automatically extended if necessary past the scheduled end time until ten minutes have passed without a bid. Roth and Ockenfels [94] study second-price auctions run by eBay and Amazon where a bidder submits a reservation price which is used to bid for him by proxy. The clear difference observed in the amount of late bidding in eBay and Amazon is strong evidence that the fixed end time gives bidders an incentive to bid late. The size of the difference between bid distributions on eBay and Amazon suggests that the different rules for ending an auction is an important element of auction design. The relation between market design and artificial agent design is discussed in [84]. The effect of different ending rules under controlled conditions are reported by Dan *et al.* [24]. The difference in auction ending rules is sufficient by itself to produce the differences in late bidding observed in the field data. The strategic advantages of late bidding are severely attenuated in auctions that apply an automatic extension rule such as auctions conducted on Amazon [85].

6.2 Time Strategies

6.2.1 Motivations

Consider a CDA market with a pre-specified fixed deadline for each round. As in Section 3.3.1, a period of thinking time elapses before an agent submits an ask or a bid. The thinking time resembles a human trader's thinking time before submitting his ask or bid in the market.

For example, as a human seller, if he knows that supply is less than demand, it means that he can easily sell most of his goods. He will prefer to wait some time before entering the trading process of the market. During the waiting time, the outstanding ask may be decreased and the outstanding bid may be increased gradually. The increased outstanding bid will improve the profit gained by the human seller if he accepts the bid after the waiting time. The decreased outstanding ask will reduce the profit gained by a seller, *i.e.* seller S, if this seller submits a valid ask and makes a transaction. However, the human seller will not act as seller S because the human seller will not conclude a transaction before the waiting time ends. After the waiting time, if there is still no transaction, then the outstanding bid might become quite profitable; however, if a transaction has already been achieved, it means that some impatient seller has accepted the less profitable outstanding bid. Therefore, by waiting some time, the profit earned by the human seller will be enhanced in general.

On the contrary, the human seller feels it is difficult to trade his goods when supply is larger than demand. Observing the ferocious competition among sellers in the market, the human seller will expedite his thinking time if possible. This kind of behaviour will help the seller gain more submission opportunities and consequently more transaction opportunities, which will generally have a positive effect on the profit gained by the seller.

Therefore in a dynamic CDA market, time strategies should be considered and adjusted according to different market situations in the CDA market with a fixed deadline. In the following, time strategies for sellers and buyers are defined.

6.2.2   Definitions of Time Strategies

Definition 6.2.1. A *time strategy with submission time $T_{s,i}$* for seller i is a behaviour as follows:

- if the current time is later than $T_{s,i}$, then the seller will submit a (soft) ask to the market;

- otherwise, the seller submits no ask.

Definition 6.2.2. A *time strategy with submission time $T_{b,j}$* for buyer j is a behaviour as follows:

- if the current time is later than $T_{b,j}$, then the buyer will submit a (soft) bid to the market;

- otherwise, the buyer submits no bid.

Consider the previous example again. For the human seller, he has two different time strategies conditioning on two different market situations. If it is easy for him to trade all his goods, the value of $T_{s,i}$ should be quite large compared with the fixed deadline. We denote the large $T_{s,i}$ as $T_{s,i}^L$. For one trading process, the human seller will not really get involved in the trading process until the current time of one round is later than $T_{s,i}^L$. Similarly for a human buyer, there is a large $T_{b,j}$ as well, denoted as $T_{b,j}^L$.

On the contrary, if it is hard for the human seller to trade his goods, the value of the submission time $T_{s,i}$ should be smaller, compared with the fixed deadline. This small value of $T_{s,i}$ is denoted as $T_{s,i}^S$, representing the thinking time of the seller before submitting his ask. Therefore the current time here refers to the elapsed time since the beginning of the thinking process. For a human buyer, a small submission time is introduced and denoted as $T_{b,j}^S$.

Time strategies characterize human traders' behaviours in the CDA markets with a fixed deadline. Nevertheless, the issues of whether the adoption of time strategies can enhance the profit of an agent in agent-based CDAs with a fixed deadline, and what kind of submission time should be adopted under different market situations, are interesting questions to be addressed. Our conjectures are as follows. If it is easy for him to make transactions, employing the time strategy with $T_{s,i}^L$ or $T_{b,j}^L$ can help the agent improve his profit. On the contrary, if it is difficult for the agent to make transactions, the agent should use the time strategy with $T_{s,i}^S$ or $T_{b,j}^S$.

Before trying to answer the above questions, we must first select a superior agent thst is known to perform well in the new market. For an agent who adopts soft asks or soft bids, we have demonstrated in Chapter 4 that such an agent can generally perform better than an agent who does not adopt soft asks or bids in continuous double auctions with a deadline of inactive interval. In this chapter, the rule of terminating each round of continuous double auctions has been changed to a fixed deadline. Therefore, we need to re-compare the performance of an agent adopting soft asks or soft bids with an agent not adopting soft asks or soft bids in the new continuous double auction markets. The experimental results below tell us which kind of agents behave better in which market environment and demonstrate the trend of the agents' profit with different submission times within time strategies under various market environments.

6.3 Illusory Seller's or Buyer's Market in CDAs with a Fixed Deadline

6.3.1 Agents Trading in CDAs with a Fixed Deadline

The continuous double auctions in this chapter are different from the basic CDAs in Section 2.2.1 in that a fixed deadline is used to terminate each round. Therefore, the performance of agents adopting soft asks or bids becomes unknown in the new CDA market. Additional experiments are needed in order to compare the agent adopting soft asks or bids with the agent not adopting soft asks or bids.

Two sets of experiments are designed to compare the performance of two kinds of agents and to observe the effect of different submission times within time strategies on the profit of sellers and buyers individually. One set is for sellers, another for buyers. For the set of experiments for sellers, we compare two kinds of sellers, X_{Soft} and X, where X can be ZI-C, ZIP, GD, CP, or A-FL in the experiments. Except for the target sellers, the other sellers are selected randomly from the other four kinds of sellers. In each set, there are two groups. In one group, the buyers are all ZI-C buyers; in the other group, the buyers are random combinations of five different kinds of buyers. The random combinations of sellers and buyers aim to simulate real-life trading.

In the set of experiments for buyers, we compare two kinds of buyers X_{Soft} and X. The other buyers are randomly selected from the other four kinds of buyers. In one group, the sellers are all ZI-C sellers while the sellers are randomly selected from five kinds of sellers in another group.

The fixed deadline to terminate a round is 20000 time units.[1] When it is easy for an agent to trade, the agent should adopt $T_{s,i}^L$. The value of $T_{s,i}^L$ is from 0 to 19000, considering the fixed deadline to end one round is 20000. On the contrary, when it is difficult for an agent to trade, the agent should adopt $T_{s,i}^S$. The thinking time that an agent allows to elapse before submitting an ask or a bid is specified as a random value within a range $[1, 2000]$. Since $T_{s,i}^S$ represents the thinking time that the target agent allows to elapse before submitting an ask or a bid and is a random value drawn from a range, denoted as $[1, T_{max\_thinking\_time}^S]$, we focus on finding the optimal range $[1, T_{max\_thinking\_time}^S]$. In the following, the results for sellers are reported first.

In Figures 6.1, 6.2, 6.3, and 6.4, the solid curve represents the profit gained by ZI-C$_{Soft}$, ZIP$_{Soft}$, GD$_{Soft}$, CP$_{Soft}$, or A-FL$_{Soft}$ agents. The dashed curve represents the profit gained by ZI-C, ZIP, GD, CP, or A-FL agents. In general, the profit of ZI-C$_{Soft}$, ZIP$_{Soft}$, GD$_{Soft}$, CP$_{Soft}$, or A-FL$_{Soft}$ agents is better than that of ZI-C, ZIP, GD, CP, or A-FL agents respectively. However, when it is hard for an agent to sell his goods, especially when supply is 25 and demand is 15, it can be seen from the two curves in the middle of Figures 6.1(b), 6.1(c), and 6.1(d) that the profit of ZIP, GD, and CP sellesr is better than that of ZIP$_{Soft}$, GD$_{Soft}$ and CP$_{Soft}$ sellers when the value of $T_{max\_thinking\_time}^S$ is smaller than or equal to 1000 time units. From the two curves in the middle of Figures 6.2(a), 6.2(b), 6.2(c), and 6.2(d), the profit of ZI-C, ZIP, GD, and CP sellers is better than that of ZI-C$_{Soft}$, ZIP$_{Soft}$, GD$_{Soft}$ and CP$_{Soft}$ sellers when the value of $T_{max\_thinking\_time}^S$ is small and especially when supply is 25 and demand is 15. Similar phenomena can be observed in Figures 6.3 and 6.4.

6.3.2   Illusory Seller's or Buyer's Market

We list the transaction rate of ZI-C, ZIP, GD, CP, and A-FL sellers when the value of $T_{max\_thinking\_time}^S$ is smaller than or equal to 1000 time units and buyers are all ZI-C buyers (shown in Figures 6.1(a), 6.1(b), 6.1(c), 6.1(d), and 6.1(e)) in Figure 6.5. As an example, ZI-C sellers have successfully traded 4521 units of goods in 1000 runs of CDAs when supply is 25, demand is 10; the maximum amount of units of goods desired by ZI-C sellers to trade in 1000 runs is $5 \times 1000 = 5000$; the value of $T_{max\_thinking\_time}^S$ is 200. Therefore the transaction rate is about $4521/5000 = 0.9042$, which is shown by the left-most column in Figure 6.5(a). It can be seen from Figures 6.5(a), 6.5(b), and 6.5(c) that when supply is 25 and demand is 10, 15, and 20, these agents can sell about 70%, 90%, and 100% of their goods respectively. However, in such supply and demand relation-

---

[1] A time unit represents the smallest thinking unit for all the agents in the experiment.

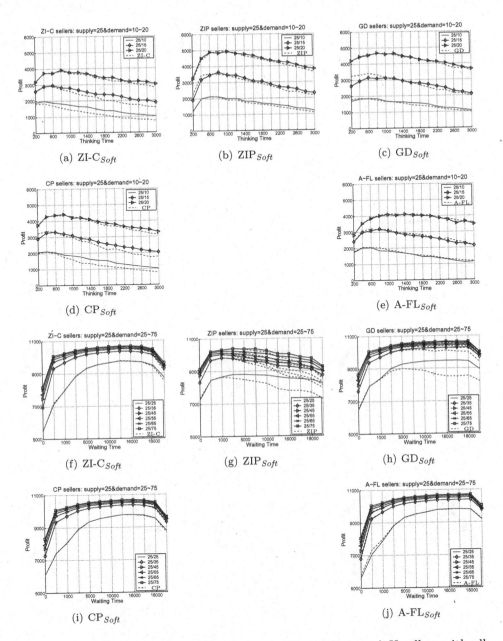

Figure 6.1: The figures in the upper part are X_{Soft} sellers and X sellers with all ZI-C buyers when supply is larger than demand. The figures in the bottom part are X_{Soft} sellers and X sellers with all ZI-C buyers when supply is smaller than or equal to demand.

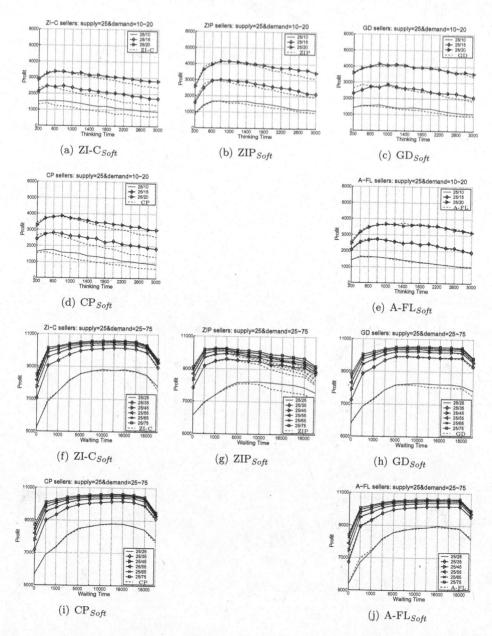

Figure 6.2: The figures in the upper part are X_{Soft} sellers and X sellers with random combination of 5 kinds of buyers when supply is larger than demand. The figures in the bottom part are X_{Soft} sellers and X sellers with random combination of 5 kinds of buyers when supply is smaller than or equal to demand.

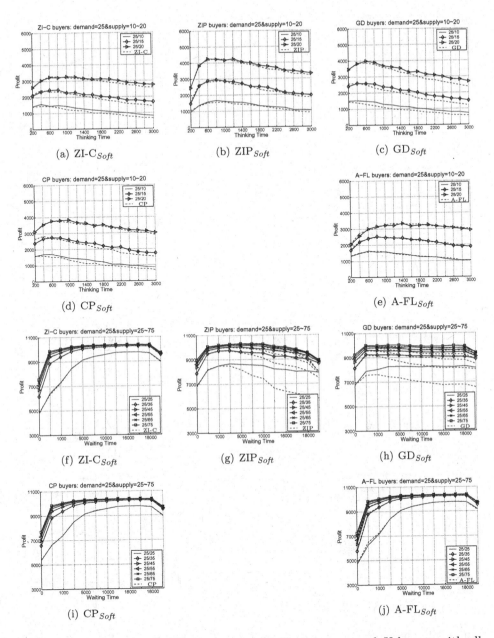

Figure 6.3: The figures in the upper part are X_{Soft} buyers and X buyers with all ZI-C sellers when demand is larger than supply. The figures in the bottom part are X_{Soft} buyers and X buyers with all ZI-C sellers when demand is smaller than or equal to supply.

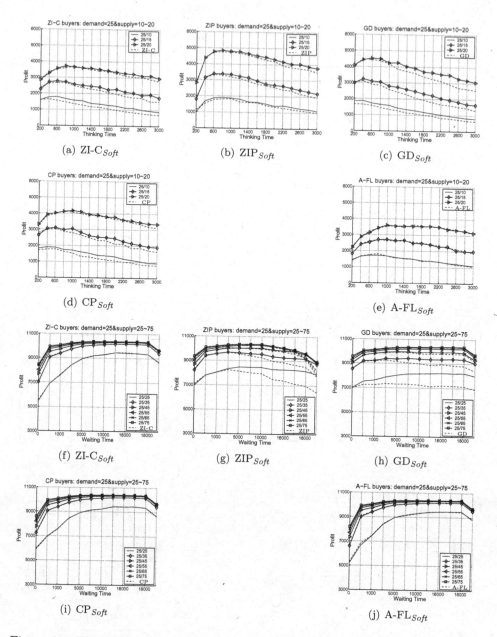

Figure 6.4: The figures in the upper part are X_{Soft} buyers and X buyers with a random combination of five kinds of sellers when demand is larger than supply. The figures in the bottom part are X_{Soft} buyers and X buyers with a random combination of five kinds of sellers when demand is smaller than or equal to supply.

ships, it should have been very difficult for an agent to sell most of his goods because in each run, 25 sellers compete for at most 10 or 15 or 20 transactions and the average transaction rate should be about 40%, 60%, and 80%. Similar results can be observed in Figure 6.6 where buyers are random combinations of various buyer agents. There is one explanation for this phenomenon as follows. When the thinking time of the X agent is generated from the range $[1, 200]$, $[1, 400]$, $[1, 600]$, $[1, 800]$, or $[1, 1000]$ while all the other agents' thinking time is generated from the range $[1, 2000]$, the X agent can gain many more submission opportunities than the other agents, which results in a large transaction amount for the agent even when supply is larger than demand. X can be ZI-C, ZIP, GD, CP, and A-FL. We call this phenomenon for sellers *"illusory seller's market"* which occurs when supply is larger than demand whilst a seller can sell most of his goods. When we explore the transaction rate of buyers, we can detect the same situation when demand is 25 and supply is 10, 15, and 20, which is called *"illusory buyer's market"*. *"illusory seller's market"* and *"illusory buyer's market"* together are called *"illusory seller's or buyer's market"* in this book.

We have so far discussed two kinds of easy selling in CDA markets. One is the illusory seller's market which happens when supply is larger than demand; another is easy selling, which occurs when supply is smaller than or equal to demand. So there arises one question: can these two kinds of easy selling be coped with in the same way? Based on the motivation of time strategies in Section 6.2, when it is easy for one agent to trade all his goods, he should wait some time before getting involved in the trading process of each round. This is reasonable for easy selling because when the seller waits under easy selling, although he will lose some submission opportunities, he will not lose transaction opportunities and his profit will not decrease since there are still enough transaction opportunities left for him. However, under the illusory seller's market when supply is larger than demand, the seller should not wait. The reason is that if the seller waits under the illusory seller's market, he will also lose some submission opportunities which will lead to fewer transactions and finally decrease the profit because there are not many transaction opportunities left for him in such a competitive market. For the illusory buyer's market, it is not the same as easy buying for the same reason. Therefore, in the following we propose circumstance-dependent softness as a strategy to handle the illusory seller's or buyer's market.

6.4 Circumstance-Dependent Softness

In the illusory seller's market situation, X sellers have already gained a large transaction amount, shown in Figure 6.5. When X sellers are replaced by X_{Soft} sellers who can make only slight compromises in this case, the profit sacrificed by making a compromise in each transaction cannot be reimbursed by a limited increase of the transaction amount. Therefore the total profit of X_{Soft} sellers may be less than or similar to the profit of X sellers because the margin left for an increase of the transaction amount is very limited.

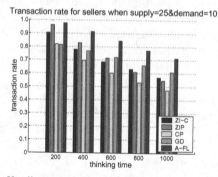

(a) X sellers when supply is 25 and demand is 10

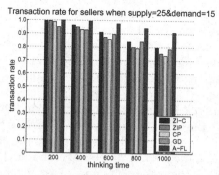

(b) X sellers when supply is 25 and demand is 15

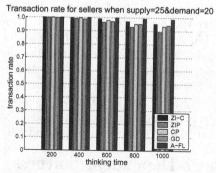

(c) X sellers when supply is 25 and demand is 20

Figure 6.5: The Y axis shows the value of the rate which is computed by the transaction amount of X sellers divided by 5000 with all ZI-C buyers when supply is larger than demand. The X axis is the value of $T^{S}_{max\_thinking\_time}$ from 200 to 1000. In each group, from the left most column to the right-most column shows the rate of ZI-C, ZIP, CP, GD, and A-FL.

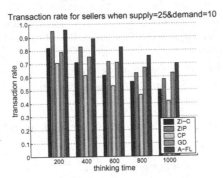

(a) X sellers when supply is 25 and demand is 10

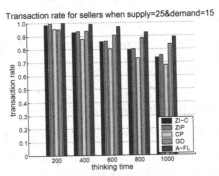

(b) X sellers when supply is 25 and demand is 15

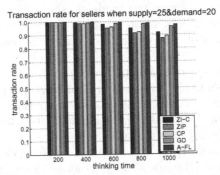

(c) X sellers when supply is 25 and demand is 20

Figure 6.6: The Y axis shows the value of the rate which is computed by the transaction amount of X sellers divided by 5000 with a random combination of buyers when supply is larger than demand. The X axis is the value of $T^S_{max\_thinking\_time}$ from 200 to 1000. In each group, from the left-most column to the right-most column shows the rate of ZI-C, ZIP, CP, GD, and A-FL.

To compensate for this shortage, the agents should increase their asks a little bit instead of decrease their asks very slightly when detecting an illusory seller's market, which introduces a negative value of δ_s and called "*circumstance-dependent negative softness*".

To incorporate circumstance-dependent negative softness, we extend soft ask and soft bid in Chapter 4 to define circumstance-dependent soft ask and soft bid as follows:

Definition 6.4.1. For a seller, a *circumstance-dependent soft ask* is a tuple (a, δ_s) such that

- if $ob > a - \delta_s$ then the seller accepts ob;

- otherwise, the seller submits a as his ask;

- δ_s can be a negative value, a positive value, or zero.

Definition 6.4.2. For a buyer, a *circumstance-dependent soft bid* is a tuple (b, δ_b) such that

- if $oa < b + \delta_b$ then the buyer accepts oa;

- otherwise, the buyer submits b as his bid;

- δ_b can be a negative value, a positive value, or zero.

We denote any strategy X integrating circumstance-dependent soft ask or bid as X_{CDS}. For agents using the previous X_{Soft} strategy, the asks or bids they submit are "softened" by adding a range to make a compromise. However, agents using X_{CDS} strategy will submit two kinds of asks or bids. Sometimes, they will submit "softened" asks or bids, similar to X_{Soft} agents. At other times, they will submit "hardened" asks or bids, which increases their profit, instead of making compromises.

Algorithms are designed for agents to adopt circumstance-dependent soft asks or bids. The codes from Line 4 to Line 5 in Figure 6.7 detect whether the current market environment is an illusory seller's market for the seller agent. If it is, δ_s is a small negative value. The seller agent should judge whether the current ob is large enough. If it is large, then the seller will accept the ob directly. Otherwise, he will submit a as his ask. If the market is not an illusory seller's market, he will submit his ask by using strategy X_{Soft} (introduced in Section 4.5.2). Similarly, the codes from Line 4 to Line 5 in Figure 6.8 first judge whether it is an illusory buyer's market for the buyer agent and then take corresponding actions.

We substitute X_{Soft} with X_{CDS} and redo the experiments in Section 6.3. The results for X_{CDS} sellers and X sellers with all ZI-C buyers are shown in Figure 6.9. The results for sellers with random combinations of different buyers are shown in Figure 6.10. It can be observed in both figures that the profit of ZI-C$_{CDS}$, ZIP$_{CDS}$, GD$_{CDS}$ and CP$_{CDS}$ sellers is obviously enhanced for different supply and demand relationships, especially when the value of $T^S_{max\_thinking\_time}$ is

---

1: calculate F_{eager};

2: ask_{amount} represents the amount of asks of all sellers from the past 10 runs to the current run;

3: bid_{amount} represents the amount of bids of all buyers from the past 10 runs to the current run;

4: **if** (F_{eager} is *close_to* 1.0) and (ask_{amount} is *larger_than* bid_{amount}) **then**

5:     δ_s is a negative value;

6:     computes a using strategy X;

7:     **if** $ob > a - \delta_s$ **then**

8:         the seller accepts ob;

9:     **else**

10:         the seller submits a as his ask;

11:     **end if**

12: **else**

13:     submits his ask by using strategy X_{Soft};

14: **end if**

Figure 6.7: The pseudo code of incorporating circumstance-dependent negative softness to sellers using strategy X.

1: calculate F_{eager};

2: ask_{amount} represents the amount of asks of all sellers from the past 10 runs to the current run;

3: bid_{amount} represents the amount of bids of all buyers from the past 10 runs to the current run;

4: **if** (F_{eager} is *close_to* 1.0) and (bid_{amount} is *larger_than* ask_{amount}) **then**

5:     δ_b is a negative value;

6:     computes b using strategy X;

7:     **if** $oa < b + \delta_b$ **then**

8:         the buyer accepts oa;

9:     **else**

10:         the buyer submits b as his bid;

11:     **end if**

12: **else**

13:     submits his bid by using strategy X_{Soft};

14: **end if**

Figure 6.8: The pseudo code of incorporating circumstance-dependent negative softness to buyers using strategy X.

between 200 and 1000 and supply is larger than demand. For these four different kinds of seller agents, when supply is 25 and demand is 20, the profit of X_{CDS} agents is enhanced more obviously than the profit achieved when supply is 25 and demand is 15 or 10. The reason is that when supply is 25 and demand is 20, illusory seller's market occurs more often, which causes the X_{CDS} seller to adopt circumstance-dependent negative softness and, in the end, improves the profit.

From Figures 6.11 and 6.12, it can be seen that an illusory buyer's market occurs and the performance of X_{CDS} buyers is greatly enhanced under various supply and demand relationships by integrating circumstance-dependent softness in general.

However, for A-FL$_{CDS}$ agents, the profit is still similar to that of A-FL agents when supply is larger than demand, shown in Figures 6.9, 6.10, 6.11, and 6.12, just like A-FL$_{Soft}$ agents and A-FL agents. The reason for this phenomenon is that A-FL sellers can compute their asks adaptively and keep a satisfied transaction frequency by adjusting risk attitude. This can be observed from Figures 6.13 and 6.14, no matter that buyers are all ZI-C buyers or a random combination of various buyers. Based on the experimental data in Figure 6.9, when supply is 25 and demand is 10, 15, or 20, the ratio of the transaction amount of A-FL sellers divided by that of A-FL$_{CDS}$ sellers is always about 1.0. However, for CP, GD, ZI-C, or ZIP sellers, this ratio is not stable to 1.0. One explanation for this difference is as follows. When circumstance-dependent softness is integrated to the A-FL agent, he will adjust the values of asks computed to counteract the effect of circumstance-dependent softness such that he can keep a similar transaction frequency compared with not integrating circumstance-dependent softness. With a similar transaction frequency and transaction amount, the profit in the end is similar. This is also true for A-FL$_{CDS}$ sellers in Figure 6.10 and A-FL$_{CDS}$ buyers in Figures 6.11 and 6.12.

6.5 Effect of Different Submission Time

On the basis of the experimental results in Section 6.4, X_{CDS} agents are illustrated to behave better than X_{Soft} agents and X agents. Therefore, we choose X_{CDS} agents as target agents in CDA markets with a fixed deadline. The questions whether the adoption of time strategies can enhance the profit of an agent using circumstance-dependent soft asks and bids, and what kind of submission time should be adopted under different market situations, can be answered according to the experimental results in the previous sections.

The solid curves in Figure 6.9(a) show the profit of ZI-C$_{CDS}$ sellers when the supply is 25 while the demand is 10, 15, and 20 from bottom to top. Since $T_{s,i}^{S}$ represents the thinking time that an agent allows to elapse before submitting an ask and is a random value drawn from a range, denoted as $[1, T_{max\_thinking\_time}^{S}]$, we focus on finding the optimal range $[1, T_{max\_thinking\_time}^{S}]$. There are many ranges to be explored, such as $[1, 200], [1, 400], [1, 600], [1, 800], [1, 1000], [1, 1200], [1, 1400]$,

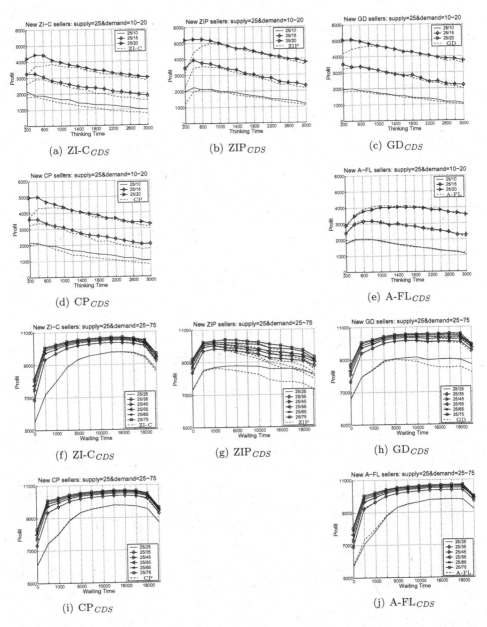

Figure 6.9: The figures in the upper part are X_{CDS} sellers and X sellers with all ZI-C buyers when supply is larger than demand. The figures in the bottom part are X_{CDS} sellers and X sellers with all ZI-C buyers when supply is smaller than or equal to demand.

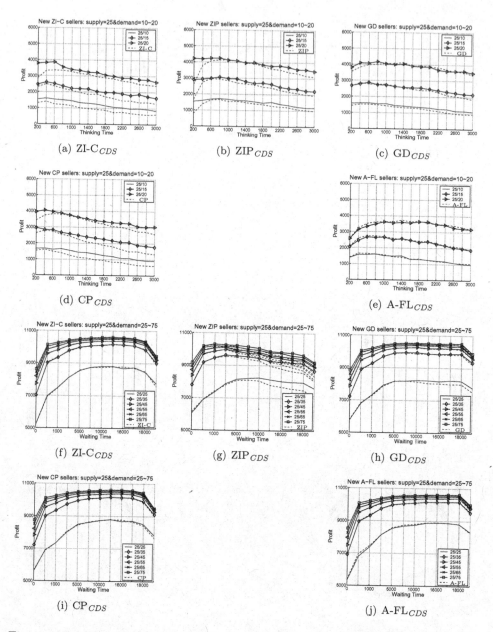

Figure 6.10: The figures in the upper part are X_{CDS} sellers and X sellers with a random combination of different buyers when supply is larger than demand. The figures in the bottom part are X_{CDS} sellers and X sellers with a random combination of different buyers when supply is smaller than or equal to demand.

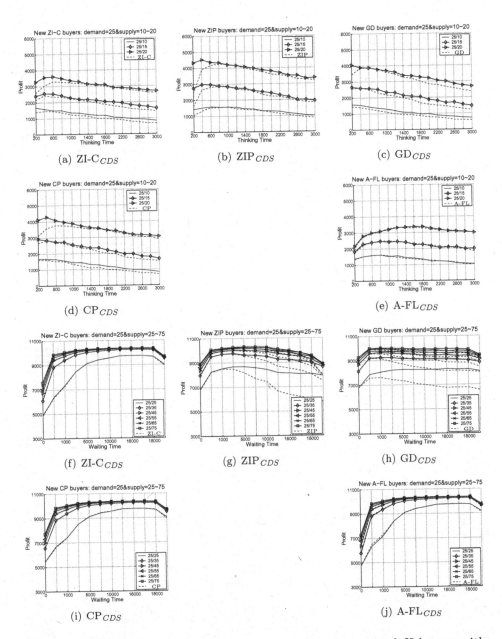

Figure 6.11: The figures in the upper part are X_{CDS} buyers and X buyers with all ZI-C sellers when demand is larger than supply. The figures in the bottom part are X_{CDS} buyers and X buyers with all ZI-C sellers when demand is smaller than or equal to supply.

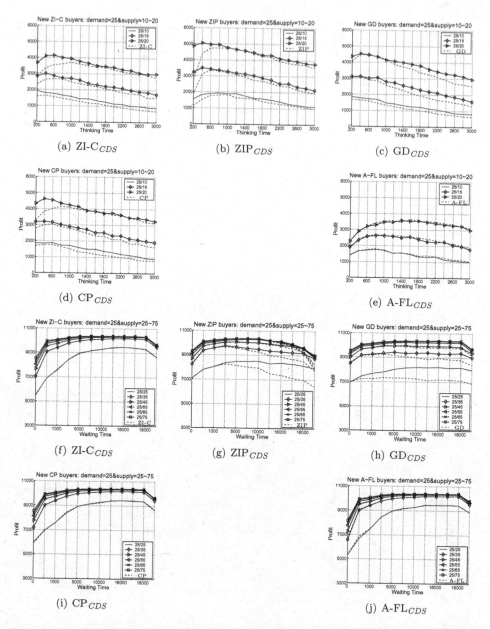

Figure 6.12: The figures in the upper part are X_{CDS} buyers and X buyers with a random combination of different sellers when demand is larger than supply. The figures in the bottom part are X_{CDS} buyers and X buyers with a random combination of different sellers when demand is smaller than or equal to supply.

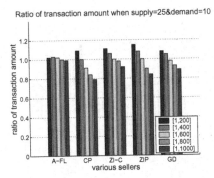

(a) X sellers when supply is 25 and demand is 10

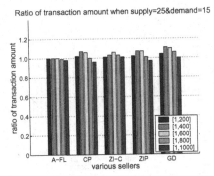

(b) X sellers when supply is 25 and demand is 15

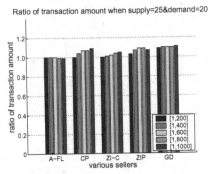

(c) X sellers when supply is 25 and demand is 20

Figure 6.13: The Y axis shows the value of the ratio which is computed by the transaction amount of X sellers divided by the transaction amount of X_{CDS} sellers with all ZI-C buyers when supply is larger than demand. In each group for any kind of agents, from the left-most column to the right-most column shows the ratio when the thinking time is generated from $[1, 200]$, $[1, 400]$, $[1, 600]$, $[1, 800]$, and $[1, 1000]$. Here X can be ZI-C, ZIP, CP, GD, or A-FL.

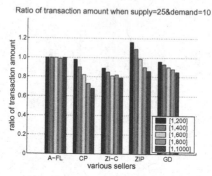

(a) X sellers when supply is 25 and demand is 10

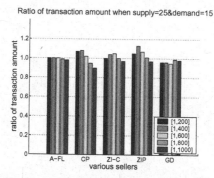

(b) X sellers when supply is 25 and demand is 15

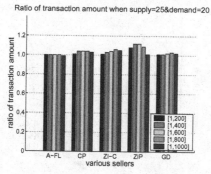

(c) X sellers when supply is 25 and demand is 20

Figure 6.14: The Y axis shows the value of the ratio which is computed by the transaction amount of X sellers divided by the transaction amount of X_{CDS} sellers with random combination of buyers when supply is larger than demand. In each group for any kind of agents, from the left-most column to the right-most column shows the ratio when the thinking time is generated from $[1, 200]$, $[1, 400]$, $[1, 600]$, $[1, 800]$, and $[1, 1000]$. Here X can be ZI-C, ZIP, CP, GD, or A-FL.

$[1, 1600]$, $[1, 1800]$, $[1, 2000]$, $[1, 2200]$, $[1, 2400]$, $[1, 2600]$, $[1, 2800]$, and $[1, 3000]$, considering that the range adopted by all the other agents in the market is $[1, 2000]$. Because all the values of $T_{s,i}^{S}$ are generated by the same method, the average thinking time generated from the range $[1, 2800]$ should be higher than the average thinking time produced from the range $[1, 2000]$. The buyers can be all ZI-C buyers or a random mixture of different buyers. It can be observed that the trend of the solid curves in Figures 6.9(b), 6.9(d), 6.9(c), and 6.9(e) are similar to the solid curve in Figure 6.9(a). A similar trend can also be found in the upper part of Figures 6.10, 6.11, and 6.12.

It can be seen from the solid curves in the upper part of Figures 6.9, 6.10, 6.11, and 6.12 that if the value of $T_{max\_thinking\_time}^{S}$ is higher than 2000, the profit of the agent is smaller than that of an agent with the range of $[1, 2000]$; otherwise, if $T_{max\_thinking\_time}^{S}$ is lower than 2000, the profit of the agent is increased gradually with the decrease of $T_{max\_thinking\_time}^{S}$ and better than the profit of an agent with the range of $[1, 2000]$, until the maximal profit is achieved; if the agent continues to decrease $T_{max\_thinking\_time}^{S}$ from the maximal point to 200, the profit may become smaller and smaller and in some cases worse than the profit of an agent with the range of $[1, 2000]$.

When the value of $T_{max\_thinking\_time}^{S}$ is higher than 2000, the average thinking time generated from $[1, T_{max\_thinking\_time}^{S}]$ is larger than the average thinking time from $[1, 2000]$. Therefore, the agent with the former range cannot get as many opportunities to submit his asks or bids as that of an agent using the latter range, which as a result reduces the profit. When the value of $T_{max\_thinking\_time}^{S}$ is smaller than 2000, the agent can get his profit enhanced because of more submissions. In particular, when the value of $T_{max\_thinking\_time}^{S}$ is very small, the agent will adopt circumstance-dependent negative softness to handle the special market situation, illusory seller's or buyer's market, and the profit will be greatly increased in general.

Figure 6.9(f) shows the profit of ZI-C$_{CDS}$ sellers with different values of $T_{s,i}^{L}$ when it is easy for a seller to sell his goods. The value of $T_{s,i}^{L}$ is from 0 to 19000, considering the fixed deadline to end one round is 20000. The supply is 25 and the demand is 25, 35, 45, 55, 65, and 75. Similar curves can be observed when ZI-C$_{CDS}$ sellers are substituted with ZIP$_{CDS}$, GD$_{CDS}$, CP$_{CDS}$, and A-FL$_{CDS}$ sellers; and when the buyers are all ZI-C buyers or a random combination of different buyers shown in the bottom part of Figures 6.9 and 6.10. If the agent just waits 500 time units, the profit can be enhanced a lot compared with the profit gained when $T_{s,i}^{L}$ is equal to 0. Then the profit continues to increase with the increase of $T_{s,i}^{L}$. The maximal profit occurs when $T_{s,i}^{L}$ is around 15000. After the maximal value, the profit will decrease step by step with the increase of $T_{s,i}^{L}$. A similar trend of buyers can be seen in the bottom part in Figures 6.11 and 6.12.

A good performance occurs when the value of $T_{s,i}^{L}$ is between 500 and 19000, which is due to the waiting behaviour brought by the time strategy. This kind of waiting has two functions helpful for profit increase. On the one hand, it lets the outstanding bid increase (outstanding ask decrease) and become more profitable for sellers (buyers). On the other hand, impatient sellers (buyers) can take those transactions achieved before the time $T_{s,i}^L$, where the outstanding bid (outstanding ask) cannot have enough chances to be updated.

Besides the trends seen from X_{CDS} agents in Figures 6.9, 6.10, 6.11, and 6.12, similar trends can be observed if we have a look at X_{Soft} agents in Figures 6.1, 6.2, 6.3, and 6.4 and X agents in Figures 6.1, 6.2, 6.3, 6.4, 6.9, 6.10, 6.11, and 6.12.

All the above phenomena confirm our conjecture in Section 6.2.2 and tell the agent that if it is easy for him to trade all his goods, he should wait some time before submitting his asks or bids to the market, and the profit can be significantly enhanced compared with not waiting at all; if the agent waits until close to the fixed deadline of ending one round, the profit will decrease and may be worse than the profit without waiting. On the contrary, when it is difficult for the agent to trade his goods, he should shorten his thinking time if possible in order to improve the profit. In particular, if he submits his asks or bids very quickly, which may cause the illusory seller's or buyer's market situation, he needs to adopt circumstance-dependent negative softness; if he takes too long a time to think, he should try to expedite his action, which will be sure to benefit him. If it is impossible for some slow agent to act quickly, then this agent should submit his asks, once determined, as soon as it becomes possible.

6.6 Adaptive Mechanisms for Sellers and Buyers to Utilize Time Strategies

In practical CDA markets, an agent does not know the current supply and demand relationship, others' reservation prices, others' threshold values, *etc.* Therefore, the principles of an adaptive mechanism that adjusts the value of submission times in the time strategies are provided on the basis of eagerness in Section 4.5.1 and the rules presented in Section 6.5.

The adaptive mechanism for sellers based on these principles is given in Figure 6.15. The seller first computes the current eagerness and initializes $T_{s,i}^L$ and $T_{max\_thinking\_time}^S$. If the current market is an illusory seller's market, the agent will adopt the circumstance-dependent negative softness, shown from line 8 to 15. Otherwise, if it is easy for him to sell most of his goods, he will adjust $T_{s,i}^L$ accordingly when the profit is in the direction of increase or decrease, shown from line 17 to line 24; if it is hard for him to sell, he will adjust $T_{max\_thinking\_time}^S$ in a parallel way shown from line 25 to line 35. The pseudo code of the adaptive mechanism for buyers using strategy X in Figure 6.16 is similar to that for sellers.

Within the pseudo code, a fuzzy set F_{eager} *is close_to 1.0* is employed, which represents the distance from the current value of F_{eager} to 1.0. λ and α are determined considering a fixed deadline. θ and β should be decided considering the

1: calculate F_{eager}; $T_{s,i}^L = \alpha$; $T_{max\_thinking\_time}^S = \beta$;
2: ask_{amount} represents the amount of asks of all the seller from the past 10 runs to the current run;
3: bid_{amount} represents the amount of bids of all the buyers from the past 10 runs to the current run;
4: T_{cur} represents the current time of the round;
5: T_{last} represents the time of the last submission of (soft) asks by seller i in the round;
6: P_2 represents the profit of seller i from the past $2m$ runs to the past m runs;
7: P_1 represents the profit of seller i from the past m runs to the current run;
8: **if** (F_{eager} is $close\_to$ 1.0) and (ask_{amount} is $larger\_than$ bid_{amount}) **then**
9:     δ_s is a small negative value;
10:     computes a using strategy X;
11:     **if** $ob > a - \delta_s$ **then**
12:         the seller accepts ob;
13:     **else**
14:         the seller submits a as his ask;
15:     **end if**
16: **else**
17:     **if** F_{eager} is $close\_to$ 1.0 **then**
18:         **if** $P_1 < P_2$ **then**
19:             $\lambda = -\lambda$;
20:         **end if**
21:         $T_{s,i}^L = T_{s,i}^L + \lambda$;
22:         **if** $T_{cur} \geq T_{s,i}^L$ **then**
23:             submits his ask by using strategy X_{Soft};
24:         **end if**
25:     **else**
26:         **if** $P_1 < P_2$ **then**
27:             $\theta = -\theta$;
28:         **end if**
29:         $T_{max\_thinking\_time}^S = T_{max\_thinking\_time}^S + \theta$;
30:         generate $T_{s,i}^S$ from $[1, T_{max\_thinking\_time}^S]$;
31:         **if** $(T_{cur} - T_{last}) == T_{s,i}^S$ **then**
32:             $T_{last} = T_{cur}$;
33:             submits his ask by using strategy X_{Soft};
34:         **end if**
35:     **end if**
36: **end if**

Figure 6.15: The pseudo code of the adaptive mechanism for sellers using strategy X.

1: calculate F_{eager}; $T_{b,j}^L = \alpha$; $T_{max\_thinking\_time}^S = \beta$;

2: ask_{amount} represents the amount of asks of all sellers from the past 10 runs to the current run;

3: bid_{amount} represents the amount of bids of all buyers from the past 10 runs to the current run;

4: T_{cur} represents the current time of the round;

5: T_{last} represents the time of the last submission of (soft) bids by buyer j in the round;

6: P_2 represents the profit of buyer j from the past $2m$ runs to the past m runs;

7: P_1 represents the profit of buyer j from the past m runs to the current run;

8: **if** (F_{eager} is $close\_to$ 1.0) and (bid_{amount} is $larger\_than$ ask_{amount}) **then**

9:      δ_b is a small negative value;

10:     computes b using strategy X;

11:     **if** $oa < b + \delta_b$ **then**

12:         the buyer accepts oa;

13:     **else**

14:         the buyer submits b as his bid;

15:     **end if**

16: **else**

17:     **if** F_{eager} is $close\_to$ 1.0 **then**

18:         **if** $P_1 < P_2$ **then**

19:             $\lambda = -\lambda$;

20:         **end if**

21:         $T_{b,j}^L = T_{b,j}^L + \lambda$;

22:         **if** $T_{cur} \geq T_{b,j}^L$ **then**

23:             submits his bid by using strategy X_{Soft};

24:         **end if**

25:     **else**

26:         **if** $P_1 < P_2$ **then**

27:             $\theta = -\theta$;

28:         **end if**

29:         $T_{max\_thinking\_time}^S = T_{max\_thinking\_time}^S + \theta$;

30:         generate $T_{b,j}^S$ from $[1, T_{max\_thinking\_time}^S]$;

31:         **if** $(T_{cur} - T_{last}) == T_{b,j}^S$ **then**

32:             $T_{last} = T_{cur}$;

33:             submits his bid by using strategy X_{Soft};

34:         **end if**

35:     **end if**

36: **end if**

Figure 6.16: The pseudo code of the adaptive mechanism for buyers using strategy X.

average thinking time of all agents. If the values of α and β are too large or small, the agent will need more time to find a suitable value. If the values of λ and θ are too large, the agent may barely maintain a suitable value. If the values of λ and θ are too small, more time is needed to find the optimal value. m is the number of runs required to record the profit. If the value of m is too large, the agent will adjust his behaviour very slowly and not be sensitive to the market changing.

6.7 Experimental Evaluation of Adaptive Mechanisms

To evaluate the performance of agents employing adaptive mechanisms, we design two sets of experiments for sellers and buyers respectively. In each set of experiments, the profit gained by X_{CDS} agents is compared with the profit gained by X_{CDS} agents incorporating adaptive mechanism, denoted as $X_{CDS,Time}$. X can be ZI-C, ZIP, GD, CP, and A-FL, which are the most widely cited strategies for agent-based CDAs in the literature.

6.7.1 Experimental Setup

In each run, a seller is endowed with a number of units of goods, reservation prices of which are independently drawn from a uniform distribution within $[1.1, 1.3]$. Similarly, the reservation prices for the units of goods needed by a buyer are independently drawn from $[3.1, 3.3]$. The thinking time that an agent allows to elapse before submitting an ask or a bid is specified as randomly distributed values within the range $[1, 2000]$. The fixed deadline to terminate a round is 20000 time units. In order to measure how well an agent performs in a CDA, we evaluate his performance by the profit he gains. For a seller i, the total profit on all s units sold in a run is $\sum_{k=1}^{s}(P_k^{(i)} - C_k^{(i)})$ where $P_k^{(i)}$ is the transaction price and $C_k^{(i)}$ is the reservation price of the unit of goods. Similarly for a buyer j, the total profit on all t units bought in a run is $\sum_{k=1}^{t}(R_k^{(j)} - P_k^{(j)})$ where $R_k^{(j)}$ is the reservation price. An agent's profit is calculated as the sum of the total profits in 1,000 runs.

The threshold for the fuzzy set is 0.9 in the experiments since the range of F_{eager} is from 0.0 to 1.0. λ is set to 100 and α is 15000 because the fixed deadline to end one round is 20000. θ is set to 20 and β is 1000, considering the average thinking time is 1000 in the market. m is set to be 10 runs since the units of goods traded in each run by each agent are about 5 units.

In each experiment for sellers, the number of units of goods desired to be sold by X_{CDS} sellers and $X_{CDS,Time}$ sellers are 5 units. All other sellers are randomly selected from a pool. In the pool, different kinds of sellers are put together and the number of units of goods for each kind is set as 10. At the beginning of each run, 15 units are randomly selected from the pool. Hence, the combination of sellers changes from time to time. The supply is always 25. The demand is altered from 10, 15, 20, 25, 35, 45, to 55 every 1000 runs.

For the set of experiments for sellers, two groups of experiments are carried out. In the first group of experiments, all the buyers are ZI-C buyers,[2] which simulates a simple CDA market. In the second group of experiments, a combination of different buyers is randomly selected from a pool of 5 kinds of buyers. Therefore, the combination of buyers is also dynamically changing. Compared with the first group, the second group resembles more of a real CDA market by allowing different kinds of buyers and sellers freely to join and leave at the beginning of each run. The experimental setup for buyers is similar to that for sellers.

6.7.2 Experimental Results for Sellers

Figures 6.17(a), 6.17(b), 6.17(c), 6.17(d), and 6.17(e) show the experimental results for $X_{CDS,Time}$ sellers with all ZI-C buyers. Figures 6.17(f), 6.17(g), 6.17(h), 6.17(i), and 6.17(j) show the results for $X_{CDS,Time}$ sellers with different buyers.

It can be observed in Figure 6.17 that the profit gained by agents using $X_{CDS,Time}$ is significantly better than that of agents using X_{CDS} when supply is smaller than demand, equal to demand, or larger than demand. The reasons are as follows. When supply is smaller than or equal to demand, it is easy for sellers to trade; a $X_{CDS,Time}$ seller will adaptively adjust the value of $T_{s,i}^L$; consequently the profit can be greatly enhanced compared with a X_{CDS} seller who does not utilize the time strategy to adjust his behaviour with the time. On the contrary, when supply is larger than demand, it is difficult for sellers to trade. A $X_{CDS,Time}$ seller will adjust the value of $T_{s,i}^S$ instead of $T_{s,i}^L$; as a result a $X_{CDS,Time}$ seller grabs more submission chances than a X_{CDS} seller and gains more profit.

Another phenomenon observed from Figure 6.17 is that when supply is 25 and demand is 20 or 25, the profit curve of $X_{CDS,Time}$ sellers is close to the curve of X_{CDS} sellers. The reason is that under these situations, the value of eagerness oscillates from 0.8 to 1.0, which reflects the real-time market fluctuation within a short time period, e.g. two consecutive runs. Because the threshold of close_to is 0.9, the $X_{CDS,Time}$ seller will switch between adjusting $T_{b,j}^L$ and adjusting $T_{b,j}^S$, which turns out to decrease the profit in some degree. If the exact supply and demand relationship can be known in advance, the result will be enhanced for this case.

In addition, it can be seen that the layout of two curves in different figures is not the same. For example, in Figures 6.17(a), 6.17(d), and 6.17(e), the thick curve is obviously further away from the slim curve. In Figures 6.17(b) and 6.17(c), these two curves are close to each other, compared with the curves in Figures 6.17(a), 6.17(d), and 6.17(e). This is understandable because in our experiments, we test the performance of five different bidding strategies, which determines the different performance. When all these various bidding strategies show the same trend of performance after incorporating the adaptive mechanism to adjust submission time in the time strategies, the robustness of the adaptive mechanisms is demonstrated.

---

[2]In [53], they also use ZI-C strategy as the benchmark strategy, which is the fair and simplest benchmark strategy.

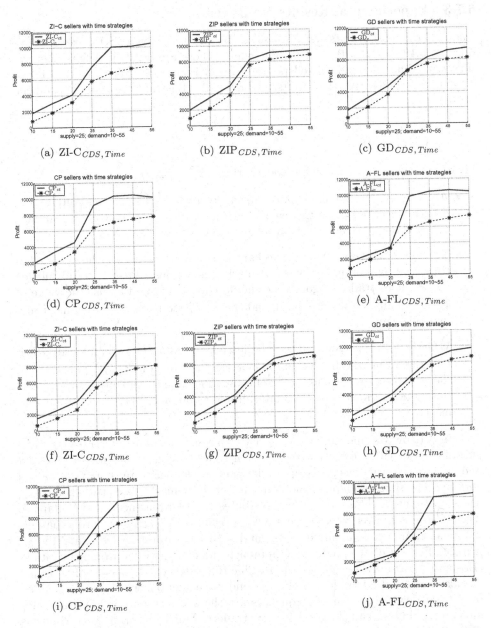

Figure 6.17: The figures in the upper part are $X_{CDS,Time}$ sellers and X_{CDS} sellers with all ZI-C buyers. The figures in the bottom part are $X_{CDS,Time}$ sellers and X_{CDS} sellers with different buyers. X_c represents X_{CDS} and X_{ct} represents $X_{CDS,Time}$.

6.7.3 Experimental Results for Buyers

The experimental results for $X_{CDS,Time}$ buyers are shown in Figures 6.18(a), 6.18(b), 6.18(c), 6.18(d), and 6.18(e) when sellers are all ZI-C sellers. The results with different kinds of sellers are given in Figures 6.18(f), 6.18(g), 6.18(h), 6.18(i), and 6.18(j). All the results for buyers demonstrate the same phenomena as sellers.

6.7.4 Discussion

There are several reasons for the good performance of $X_{CDS,Time}$ agents.

- An adaptive mechanism enables an agent to learn the current supply and demand situation from the agent's own point of view. The core is eagerness which is demonstrated to be a reliable guidance for the agent.

- The agent with an adaptive mechanism can learn to adjust the submission time step by step under different market situations. When it is difficult for the agent to trade his goods, he should choose $T_{s,i}^L$ and adjust the value of $T_{s,i}^L$ gradually. Otherwise, he should choose $T_{s,i}^S$ to begin the adjustment in a dynamic way.

- When $T_{s,i}^L$ ($T_{s,i}^S$) is selected to be adjusted, several rules are employed, which tells the agent whether he should increase the value of $T_{s,i}^L$ ($T_{s,i}^S$) or decrease the value according to his record of profit. Through this adaptive adjustment, the agent can always find a more suitable value of $T_{s,i}^L$ ($T_{s,i}^S$) for the current market.

In [71] by Ma and Leung, X_{Soft} agents are employed to illustrate the time effect in CDAs with a fixed deadline. Similar trends of time strategies are observed and similar adaptive mechanisms are designed to demonstrate that X_{Soft} agents adopting the similar adaptive mechanisms behave remarkably better then X_{Soft} agents without it. This work also contributes to the robustness of the adaptive mechanisms no matter whether we use X_{Soft} agent or X_{CDS} agent in this chapter.

Our approach is mainly experimental with laboratorial experiments. In [94] [84] [24], Roth et al. took a different approach and demonstrated from field data in eBay and Amazon online auctions in real life that late bidding is not only rational but also beneficial for traders in eBay second-price auctions which are terminated by a fixed deadline. Their consequences are the same as ours in that late submission of bidding can do good for the traders. Moreover, their work confirms the motivation of late submission of our work based on real-life data in eBay and Amazon. Our work provides the whole trend of the effect of different submission times to the trader agent when it is easy for him to trade his goods. In addition, our work supports the contention that, when it is difficult for the agent to trade, the agent should try to shorten his thinking time if possible with the dynamic

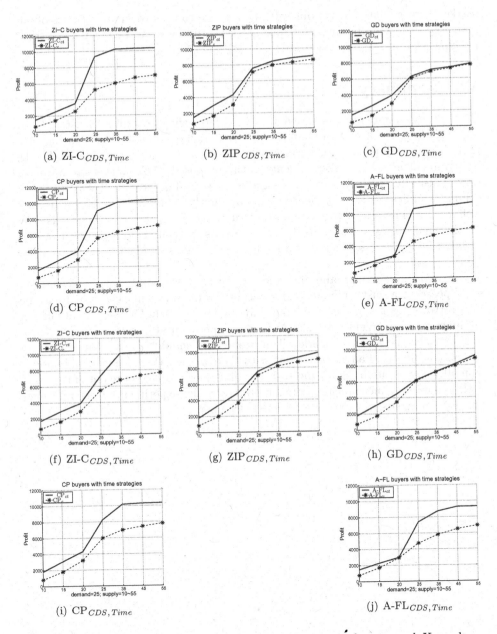

Figure 6.18: The figures in the upper part are $X_{CDS,Time}$ buyers and X_{CDS} buyers with all ZI-C sellers. The figures in the bottom part are $X_{CDS,Time}$ buyers and X_{CDS} buyers with different sellers. X_c represents X_{CDS} and X_{ct} represents $X_{CDS,Time}$.

market environment. Hence, our work tries to capture more characteristics of human traders in real life under various market situations and illustrates the trend by experimental results in the lab.

6.8 Summary

Usually, any trading process in real life is associated with a deadline. Existing CDA mechanisms in the literature do not consider a fixed deadline for terminating each round. In this chapter, a CDA market with a fixed deadline is considered. Unlike agents in other CDA markets, agents in the proposed CDA market are aware of time. Naturally, they will spend the time to think and determine at which time to submit their asks or bids. Time strategies are firstly defined to express the agent's feeling with time under various market situations. The rules are: when it is easy for the agent to trade his goods, he should wait some time before getting involved in the trading process; when it is difficult to trade, he should shorten his thinking time if possible.

Based on eagerness and the rules explored above, an adaptive mechanism is proposed to adjust time strategies within the unknown market, which can be integrated by agents utilizing different bidding strategies in CDAs and submitting circumstance-dependent soft asks and bids. Experimental results show that when it is easy for the agent to trade all his goods, he should adopt a large value of submission time and adjust the value with the market; otherwise he should adopt a small value of submission time to begin. The performance of agents integrated with an adaptive mechanism is demonstrated by the experiments to significantly outperform agents without an adaptive mechanism.

Chapter 7

Discussion of the Results

Given the results from the previous chapters, one may want to know how these results can be applied in real-life CDA markets. In order to answer this question, we shall in this chapter highlight the differences between the real-life CDA markets and the agent-oriented CDA markets researched in this book. We then provide an overall discussion on the results observed from these agent-oriented CDA markets, focusing on the scenarios where the results are applicable.

7.1 The Characteristics of Agent Oriented CDAs

In the basic CDA market described in Section 2.2.1, there are only a limited number of sellers and buyers trading a limited amount of goods, which means that the supply and the demand are limited. Consequently, if a seller increases his ask, every other agent in the market can observe, and use it to help determine his own ask or bid in the current round. If the seller can still make a transaction after increasing his ask, this means that there are some buyers who are willing to accept it. This transaction price will consequently affect other agents' decisions in the future rounds. Therefore, the behaviour of a seller or buyer can have observable direct influence on the market situation. Besides, all the sellers and buyers in the market are trading homogeneous goods. In each round of the CDAs, at most one unit of the homogeneous goods is traded. We call a CDA market which has a limited supply and demand and allows one unit of the homogeneous goods to be traded in one round a *small-scale CDA market*.

The motivation to focus on such small-scale CDA markets is as follows. Generally speaking, CDA markets present some distinct advantages as the basis for trading agent research, including low barriers to entry, consensus understanding of market rules, and opportunity to build upon prior work, *etc.* In particular, small-scale CDA markets have served as a basis for many studies of artificial trading agents since they well model some real-life CDA markets, and they are challenging and interesting. Unlike research on large-scale CDA markets, which can make use of (real-life) past data for evaluation of newly proposed bidding strategies, most research on small-scale CDA markets are done by experiments and simulations in which every participating agent's actions have an immediate effect on other agents' decision process and the market itself [102], [42], [22], [17], [21], [92], [41], [108], [107], [53], [86], [116].

Real-life CDA markets come in various forms, each of which has distinct characteristics. One form of the CDA variants used for real-world trading is the persistent shout double auction [89]. Fastparts [1] is such a marketplace on the Internet, which provides a persistent shout double auction for buying and selling overstocked electronic components. In the Fastparts marketplace, after the highest bid is matched with the lowest ask, they are deleted from the market and then the remaining agents can continue trading until all agents have bought or sold all they desire to buy or sell. Therefore multiple transactions can take place in one round — which is not permitted in the small-scale CDA market.

Another example is the New York Stock Exchange (NYSE) which also uses a form of persistent shout double auction. The NYSE rule states that the current bid and ask persist, and any new bid or ask must improve on the existing one [88], [43], [22]. The main characteristic of the CDAs adopted by NYSE is that there are a huge number of buyers and sellers in this auction market. The behaviour of an individual seller or buyer cannot change the trend of the market and cannot even affect the behaviours of other sellers and buyers.[2] Therefore when researchers carry out research in the stock market, they can make the assumption that individual behaviour will not change the performance of the whole stock market. Moreover, in the stock market, there are plenty of various types of stocks for agents to choose at any time and these various types of stocks can be looked on as heterogeneous goods to be traded [119], [31]. All these are fundamentally different from the small-scale CDA market focused on in this book.

Besides the above applications in real life, CDA markets have been involved in the "travel agent" scenario of the Trading Agent Competition (TAC Classic) [124]. The TAC travel-shopping market game presents a travel-shopping task, where traders assemble flights, hotels, and entertainment tickets into itineraries for a set of eight clients. Clients are described by their preferred arrival and departure days, the premium they are willing to pay to stay at a fine hotel, and their respective values for three different types of entertainment events. The agents competing in TAC are travel agents serving their clients, with the objective being to maximize the value of trips for those clients. The three categories of goods, air tickets, hotel stay, and entertainment tickets, are exchanged through distinct market mechanisms. In the entertainment ticket market, CDAs are adopted. Agents receive an initial random allocation of entertainment tickets. They then allocate the tickets to their own clients or sell to other agents in the CDA markets. Several

---

[1] http://www.fastparts.com/.

[2] The only exception here might be if an individual seller or buyer has the overwhelming ability to trade a huge amount of stocks such that the transaction price of the whole stock market is influenced. However, this is not the usual case for most individual traders in the stock markets.

trading agents have been developed to implement the strategies designed for this CDA market [48], [49], [109], [59]. The adoption of the CDA mechanism in TAC can be seen as an attempt at putting CDAs into application.

In recent years, electronic markets have come to represent an application of information systems that has generated significant new trading opportunities while allowing for the dynamic pricing of goods. Although CDAs have been the principal trading format in U.S. financial institutions for over a hundred years [1], they are rarely found in these online markets. In a nutshell, the eBay auction protocol is a variant of ascending price auctions with a minimum bid increment and a fixed closing time. Buyers interested in bidding within an auction must specify the maximum amount that they are willing to bid [93]. For other online auction websites, such as Yahoo!, Taobao, Google, *etc.*, none of them chooses CDA as an online market.

Hence we come to the conclusion that CDA is not a popular choice in real life. There are many reasons for such a phenomenon. First of all, the CDA market rule is more complicated compared with English auctions, Vickrey auctions, Dutch auctions, *etc.* Second, CDA appears to be too complex a game to yield a clear game-theoretic solution, especially for small-scale CDAs. It is hard to predict how traders will behave in this kind of market given that there is no dominant strategy, which stimulates the development of various types of bidding strategies. However, this may prevent a market organizer from choosing CDA because the organizer cannot precisely predict the behaviour of traders and the outcome of the market. As a result, this has restricted the use of CDA markets in real life.

Nevertheless, CDA is a potential choice in reality since it allows human sellers and buyers to bargain and compromise. In addition, CDA has been shown to be a highly efficient protocol [41]. Generally speaking, CDA markets produce very efficient allocations and prices [29], and the transaction prices often converge to a competitive equilibrium price.[3] We believe that all these advantages encourage industries and researchers to consider and adopt various types of CDAs and put them into use.

7.2 Scenarios in Which Results Can Be Applied

In the following, we briefly discuss some scenarios in which different strategies and tools explored in this book are applicable.

Eagerness is the core of adaptivity for AA strategy and for the tools proposed in this book in a dynamic and uncertain market environment. Given the characteristics of small-scale CDA markets, each agent trading in this market will be influenced by the behaviour of other agents and of himself as well. For example, if an agent finds that he can still make a transaction after increasing his ask, this means that some buyers are interested in his price and the demand for this good is strong enough. Then the agent will become eager to increase his asks for more

---

[3] The competitive equilibrium price is determined by the intersection of the supply and demand curves of the market [87].

profit in future rounds. Otherwise, the agent will be eager for more transaction opportunities in return for more profit in the future, because he starts to feel that his ask is not competitive and the demand for this good is not strong. This feeling will continue to be developed and adjusted throughout a series of rounds. Restricted by the incomplete information available from others and from the market protocol described in Section 2.2.1, the agent is not assumed to know the exact supply and demand in the market. However, the agent will form a feeling towards the relationship of the supply and the demand according to the information available to him through the trading process. Eagerness, defined in 3.1 and then refined in Section 4.5.1, represents such a feeling and has been used to reflect the current supply and demand relationship of dynamic market from the agent's own point of view. The value of eagerness is computed according to the agent's trading record of the short term and of the long term in a series of trading competitions. Eagerness takes effect not only in small-scale CDA markets but also in other types of markets where a series of trading competitions occurs and the behaviour of individual agents can influence one another. It has been shown that use of eagerness works well in CDAs [73], [68], [70], [71] and in some repeated single-sided auctions,[4] *e.g.*, repeated English auctions as well [72].

AA strategy developed in Chapter 3 is formed on the basis of eagerness. In order to adjust his trading behaviour with the dynamic market environment, an agent using AA strategy makes use of eagerness as his summary impression of the dynamic environment to determine his asks or bids. AA strategy computes eagerness based on the trading record of the agent, and uses it, together with the agent's private information, such as the reservation price, to compute the value of ask or bid to be submitted. With the use of eagerness, AA strategy will work well in the markets where repeated trading competitions take place and each individual agent's behaviour can influence the whole market. In [67], [73], [72], AA strategy has been demonstrated to perform well in dynamic small-scale CDA markets and repeated English auctions.

For other strategies found in the literature, such as GD, ZIP, CP, A-FL, and ZI-C, different strategies work efficiently in different scenarios. For example, ZI-C strategy (described in Section 2.3.1) computes a random value as the ask or bid to be submitted, based only on the reservation price and the acceptable price range of the market. Therefore, it can easily be used, though generally not a good choice, in a broad range of market scenarios, such as single-sided auctions, double-sided auctions,[5] auctions with a sequence of rounds, auctions in a single round, or other types of auctions. ZI-C has been widely adopted as a benchmark in the literature for the evaluation of the effectiveness of other strategies [22], [41], [53], [73], [4], [72].

---

[4]In *single-sided auctions*, there is a single seller and multiple buyers submitting their bids or a single buyer and multiple sellers submitting their asks [130]. For example, English auction, first-price sealed bid auction, second-price sealed bid auction, and Dutch auction belong to single-sided auctions.

[5]In *double-sided auctions*, there are multiple sellers and multiple buyers to trade simultaneously from both sides [130]. CDA is the most common variety of double-sided auction.

ZIP and CP strategies rely on information from the most recent round to compute asks and bids. GD and A-FL strategies require the trading record not only in the last round but in the previous several consecutive rounds. Hence, for any auction market that consists of several rounds and which can directly or indirectly provide the outstanding ask, and the outstanding bid, the transaction price, ZIP, CP, GD, and A-FL strategies can work well and adapt through the trading process. In previous work, all these strategies have been shown to perform well in CDAs [42], [22], [41], [90], [53], [73]. Moreover, ZI-C, ZIP, CP, GD, and A-FL strategies have been demonstrated to work well in repeated English auctions [72]; ZI-C, ZIP, and GD strategies have been successfully applied in repeated first-price sealed-bid auctions and repeated Vickrey auctions [4].

In addition to strategies, several tools have been introduced in Chapters 4, 5, and 6. These tools can be adopted by agents in certain market scenarios. In Section 4.2, soft asks and soft bids are introduced. The idea is to enable the agent to make compromises after his computation of asks or bids is finished, which simulates the human trader's desire to make compromises in real-life markets. First proposed by He and Leung [52], this concept can be widely used in auction scenarios where sellers/buyers can make compromises with buyers/sellers in return for more profit. It has been shown that if the degree of softness is adjusted by eagerness, use of soft asks and soft bids in ZI-C, ZIP, GD, A-FL, and CP can enhance the performance of agents in dynamic CDA markets [68].

Another tool is judgement of price acceptability, defined in Section 5.2, which means that an agent makes judgement on the asks and the bids such that he declines poor offers and accepts profitable offers without hesitation. This can prevent the agent from being trapped into poor transaction prices and losing profit, and at the same time help the agent to grab profitable transaction prices to gain more profit. Adaptive judgement of price acceptability is a strategy that agents can adopt in a dynamic market environment where a series of trading competitions takes place. This tool can be used to enhance the agent's effectiveness in both double-sided auction markets (CDA, *etc.*) and repeated single-sided auction markets (English auction, Dutch auction, Vickrey auction, first-price sealed-bid auctions, *etc.*). In [70], judgement of price acceptability has been shown to work effectively in CDAs by improving the performance of agents adopting ZI-C, ZIP, GD, A-FL, and CP.

Finally, adaptive time strategies are provided as a tool to be utilized by agents in CDAs with a fixed deadline. In such markets, agents know the time and hence know how far off the deadline is. Time strategies help an agent adjust his trading behaviour according to time, as defined in Section 6.2. In short, the agent with time strategies knows when he should submit his ask or bid to the market and when he should wait on the market. Whether it is a single-sided auction market or a double-sided auction market, the concept of time strategies is useful for agents. As an example, in CDA markets, the rules for using adaptive time strategies are explored, which is shown to greatly enhance the performance of agents using ZI-C, ZIP, GD, A-FL, and CP strategies [71].

Chapter 8

Conclusions and Future Work

8.1 Conclusions

With the increasing automation of e-commerce, we believe that ever greater amounts of trading will be conducted in online auctions by software agents. However, to make progress in this area, one of the key problems that needs to be addressed is that of developing effective and efficient bidding strategies or enhancing existing strategies that agents can use to achieve their negotiation objective. To this end, we develop novel strategies and general tools for continuous double auctions.

In particular, we first developed a strategy that guides an agent's buying and selling behaviour in a series of CDAs. The strategy, named AA strategy, uses heuristic rules and a reasoning mechanism based on two-level adaptive attitudes and the α-ω method to decide what bids or asks to place and to accept. Eagerness is defined based on the short-term attitude and the long-term attitude, which reflects the real-time supply and demand relation from an agent's point of view. The α-ω method is integrated within the heuristic rules, which tells an agent if an ask or a bid is profitable enough, then he should accept the ask or bid directly; otherwise he should decline the ask or bid immediately. We benchmarked the performance of AA strategy against six other prominent alternatives in the literature. The experiments were composed of two groups, those to simulate static CDA markets, and those to simulate dynamic CDA markets, both of which illustrates that AA strategy is the best. These results also demonstrate the importance of eagerness based on two-level adaptive attitudes and the α-ω method with heuristic rules. This result is especially promising since the benchmark strategies we evaluated against have been shown to outperform human bidders in experimental settings [25].

Based on the success of our work in CDAs, we notice that there are two kinds of behaviours contributing much to the good performance of agents. One is softness, another is judgement of price acceptability.

We introduced soft asks and soft bids for agents in CDAs. Experimental results and analysis illustrate that, when agents can trade all their units of goods, they should not adopt soft asks or bids. When agents cannot trade all their units of goods, the adoption of soft asks or bids can benefit them. When the agent finds it difficult to make a transaction, he should increase the degree of softness; otherwise, he should decrease it. In order to guide agents to adopt soft asks or bids in a dynamic CDA market, an adaptive mechanism to adjust the degree of softness was presented. We reinforce eagerness in AA strategy by employing a fuzzy set and fuzzy logic-based approach to compute the value of eagerness.

The judgement of price acceptability is introduced for sellers and buyers. The effect of the judgement of price acceptability to different kinds of strategies were investigated. Experimental results demonstrated that the adoption of the judgement of price acceptability can enhance the performance of agents. When a buyer experiences the change from easy trading of all his goods to difficult trading of some goods, the thresholds of price acceptability will accordingly change from below the average transaction price of the market to above the average transaction price. For sellers, the result is similar. According to the results and eagerness, an adaptive mechanism on the judgement of price acceptability is proposed to enable agents to decide whether oa or ob is acceptable or not before the agents calculate their asks or bids.

Experiments on agents utilizing ZI-C, ZIP, GD, A-FL, and CP with the adaptive mechanism of adjusting softness and the judgement of price acceptability have been carried out respectively. Compared with agents without that adaptive mechanism, the performance of agents with the adaptive mechanism is remarkably enhanced in various environments in general, where both the supply and demand relationship and the combination of agents are changing.

All the above work focuses on continuous double auctions with a deadline of inactive interval. However, in real-world trading, it is often essential to conclude a transaction among agents under a fixed deadline. Time strategies of agents are defined for buyers and sellers in CDAs with a fixed deadline, according to which agents can arrange their behaviours. The effect of different time strategies on the profit of agents submitting circumstance-dependent soft asks and bids was evaluated experimentally. It is shown that when it is easy for the agent to trade most of his goods, he should wait some time before getting involved in the trading process; on the contrary, he should make a quicker decision before each time to submit his bid; in particular, when an illusory seller's or buyer's market occurs, circumstance-dependent negative softness should be adopted. An adaptive mechanism is designed to guide agents employing various bidding strategies to consider the effect of time. Experimental results demonstrate that agents with the adaptive mechanism perform better than agents without the adaptive mechanism.

Through the work in this book, AA strategy has been demonstrated to be superior in a wide range of CDA scenarios. In addition, three kinds of adaptive behaviours have been shown to greatly enhance the performance of the widely adopted strategies in CDAs.

In order to clarify how to put these results into practical use, the main characteristics of the CDA market we have used in this book are discussed and the differences between the CDA market in this book and those in reality are emphasized. All the results obtained in this book are related to which market scenarios they are suitable to be applied in.

8.2 Possible Future Research Directions

When taken together, these contributions make an important step towards improving adaptivity of agents in CDAs. Despite these achievements, more work can be conducted in the future. There are several promising directions for further research based on this book:

- One interesting scenario is when agents are under time pressure to close a deal. They must adjust their bidding strategy to take time into account. Hence, market designers should consider how to incorporate time when designing CDA markets, and agents should learn how to adjust their behaviours with time in such a new market environment with a deadline [71]. There are more interesting questions related to time strategies to be addressed. When it is easy (or difficult) for the agent to trade, if all the agents utilize the same time strategies, what will the performance of the agent be? Is the mechanism still desirable and efficient? In addition, we are interested in investigating more on time strategies in other types of auctions, *e.g.*, combinatorial auctions.

- For agents adopting circumstance-dependent soft asks or soft bids, it is shown that when encountering an illusory seller's or buyer's market, circumstance-dependent negative softness should be adopted. However, we only consider a fixed circumstance-dependent negative softness in the current work. To utilize circumstance-dependent negative softness more efficiently, we may delve deeper into the relationships between the degree of circumstance-dependent negative softness and various supply and demand relationships of the market. Furthermore, we have demonstrated that circumstance-dependent negative softness is useful in handling an illusory seller's or buyer's market. Encouraged by this success, we think circumstance-dependent negative softness can be utilized in easy trading and rules can be explored as well.

- We assume that each agent wishes to trade exactly one unit of homogeneous goods in one round. However, in reality, the intention to buy or sell goods can arrive at any time, asynchronously, and sellers may desire to sell multiple units of the goods while buyers may need to purchase more than one unit of goods in each round. This requires the CDA market to support the trading of possibly more than one unit of goods in one round. Further, in real markets, people may aim to trade heterogeneous goods instead of homogeneous goods. Such features are not captured in the current strategies for CDA markets.

- Normally, bidding strategies which are designed for CDAs, such as GD, ZIP, CP, A-FL, AA, ZI-C, *etc.*, are seldom applied to other types of auctions, especially single-sided auctions, due to the differences in information revelation and allocation processes in these auction types. Bagnall and Toft [4] have tried to revise GD and ZIP strategy to be used in FPSB and SPSB auctions. They demonstrate that it is possible to utilize these adaptive strategies originally designed for CDAs in single-sided auctions, *e.g.*, repeated English auctions [72], to improve the performance of the bidding agents.

- In this work, agents are assumed to play either the role of sellers or buyers all the time in the CDA market. However, in real-life markets, agents may trade as sellers in one market while buyers in another, or even the same market. This is the key to making money from trading. For example, in the stock market, one will buy some stocks and sell them later. It will be interesting if agents can be designed to be able to do this.

- Eagerness has been widely utilized in this work. The aim of eagerness is to guide an agent to behave adaptively according to the current market environment. To form eagerness, the continuous double auction needs to be repeated for a certain period. The basic ideas of eagerness can be easily extended to other auction protocols, (*e.g.*, multiple auctions, repeated Dutch auctions, repeated English auctions, and repeated Vickrey auctions [106]), because all these auctions are characterized by repeated auctions. Furthermore, there may exist alternative ways to express eagerness in such complex and dynamic markets.

- The two kinds of adaptive behaviours, namely softness of asks or bids and judgement of price acceptability, turn out to be a great success in dynamic CDAs, which are full of uncertainties and fluctuation. Such uncertainties and fluctuation can also be observed in other types of auctions, such as repeated English auctions, combinatorial auctions, *etc.*, in which softness of asks or bids and judgement of price acceptability may also be adopted to enhance agents' performance. Some modifications may be needed because the bidding behaviours in these auctions are probably different from those in CDAs.

- In our current work, the reservation prices are randomly generated from a fixed range for various agents at the beginning of the CDA markets. Nevertheless, this is not always true in reality. It is well observed that the reservation price for one unit of goods in a local market can change according to supply and demand in a global market environment. For example, if you are the first one to sell a new high-tech product in a local market and in the global market as well, then your profit is usually quite high. However, if after one year, you are still selling the same product in the local market while there are a lot of others selling the same types of product (or, usually, better models) in other markets, then your profit will drop. In view of the depreciation of goods over time, we think it is more practical to consider the change of reservation prices dynamically with the market situation.

- In the experiments, we assume that the supply and the demand are not changed abruptly, *e.g.*, by breaking news, and prices are not affected by external factors such as rumours or individual's irrational behaviours (*e.g.*, due to prejudice). In reality, however, supply, demand and bidders' decisions can sometimes suddenly change with circumstances. Agents must be able to sense these changes, and deal with them.

Bibliography

[1] Agorics. http://www.agorics.com/Library/Auctions/auction6.html.

[2] S. Airiau, S. Sen, and G. Richard. Strategic bidding for multiple units in simultaneous and sequential auctions. In *Proceedings of the 36th Annual Hawaii International Conference on System Sciences*, Washington, DC, USA, 2003. IEEE Computer Society.

[3] R. Axelrod. *The Evolution of Cooperation*. New York: Basic Books, 1984.

[4] A. Bagnall and I. Toft. Autonomous adaptive agents for single seller sealed bid auctions. *Autonomous Agents and Multi-Agent Systems*, 12(3):259–292, 2006.

[5] R. Bapna, P. Goes, and A. Gupta. Insights and analysis of online auctions. *Communications of the ACM*, 44(11):42–50, 2001.

[6] C. Beam and A. Segev. Automated negotiation: A survey of the state of the art. *CITM Working Paper 96-WP-1022*, 1996.

[7] K. Binmore. *Fun and games: a text on game theory*. D. C. Heath, 1992.

[8] A. Birk. Boosting cooperation by evolving trust. *Applied Artificial Intelligence*, 14(8):769–784, 2000.

[9] A. Byde, C. Preist, and N. R. Jennings. Decision procedures for multiple auctions. In *Proceedings of the 1st International Joint Conference on Autonomous Agents and Multiagent Systems*, pages 613–620, New York, NY, USA, 2002. ACM.

[10] D. Cao and L. Xu. A negotiation model of incomplete information under time constraints. In *Proceedings of the 1st International Joint Conference on Autonomous Agents and Multiagent Systems*, pages 128–134, New York, NY, USA, 2002. ACM.

[11] M. Cary, A. Das, B. Edelman, I. Giotis, K. Heimerl, A. R. Karlin, C. Mathieu, and M. Schwarz. Greedy bidding strategies for keyword auctions. In *Proceedings of the 8th ACM Conference on Electronic Commerce*, pages 262–271, New York, NY, USA, 2007. ACM.

[12] C. Castelfranchi and R. Falcone. Trust and control: A dialectic link. *Applied Artificial Intelligence*, 14(8):799–823, 2000.

[13] D. Catalano and R. Gennaro. New efficient and secure protocols for verifiable signature sharing and other applications. *Journal of Computer and System Sciences*, 61(1):51–80, 2000.

[14] K. Chakravarti, E. Greenleaf, A. Sinha, A. Cheema, J. C. Cox, D. Friedman, T. H. Ho, R. M. Isaac, A. A. Mitchell, A. R., M. H. Rothkopf, J. Srivastava, and R. Zwick. Auctions: Research opportunities in marketing. *Marketing Letters*, 13(3):281–296, 2002.

[15] S. P. M. Choi and J. Liu. A dynamic mechanism for time-constrained trading. In *Proceedings of the 5th International Conference on Autonomous Agents*, pages 568–575, New York, NY, USA, 2001. ACM.

[16] D. Cliff. Evolution of market mechanism through a continuous space of auction-types. Technical Report HPL-2001-326, Bristol, UK, 2001.

[17] D. Cliff. Evolutionary optimization of parameter sets for adaptive software-agent traders in continuous double auction markets. Technical Report HPL-2001-99, Bristol, UK, 2001.

[18] D. Cliff. Evolution of market mechanism through a continuous space of auction-types ii: Two-sided auction mechanisms evolve in response to market shocks. Technical Report HPL-2002-128, Bristol, UK, 2002.

[19] D. Cliff. Evolution of market mechanism through a continuous space of auction-types iii: Multiple market shocks give convergence toward cda. Technical Report HPL-2002-312, Bristol, UK, 2002.

[20] D. Cliff. Explorations in evolutionary design of online auction market mechanisms. Technical Report HPL-2003-80, Bristol, UK, 2003.

[21] D. Cliff. Zip60: an enhanced variant of the zip trading algorithm. In *Proceedings of 2006 IEEE Joint Conference on E-Commerce Technology and Enterprise Computing, E-Commerce and E-Services*, Washington, DC, USA, June 2006. IEEE Computer Society.

[22] D. Cliff and J. Bruten. Minimal-intelligence agents for bargaining behaviors in market-based environments. Technical Report HP-97-91, Bristol, UK, Aug. 1997.

[23] P. Cramton, Y. Shoham, and R. Steinberg. *Combinatorial Auctions*. MIT Press, 2006.

[24] A. Dan, A. Ockenfels, and A. E. Roth. An experimental analysis of ending rules in internet auctions. *Rand Journal of Economics*, 36(4):891–908, 2005.

[25] R. Das, J. E. Hanson, J. O. Kephart, and G. Tesauro. Agent-human interactions in the continuous double auction. In *Proceedings of the International Joint Conference on Artificial Intelligence*, pages 1169–1176, Seattle, USA.

[26] E. David, R. Azoulay-Schwartz, and S. Kraus. Bidders' strategy for multi-attribute sequential english auction with a deadline. In *Proceedings of the 2nd International Joint Conference on Autonomous Agents and Multiagent Systems*, pages 457–464, New York, NY, USA, 2003. ACM.

[27] M. Dumas, L. Aldred, G. Governatori, and A. Hofstede. Probabilistic automated bidding in multiple auctions. *Electronic Commerce Research*, 5:25–49, 2005.

[28] M. Dumas, L. Aldred, G. Governatori, A. ter Hofstede, and N. Russell. A probabilistic approach to automated bidding in alternative auctions. In *Proceedings of the 11th International Conference on World Wide Web*, pages 99–108, New York, NY, USA, 2002. ACM.

[29] D. Easley and J. Ledyard. Theories of price formation and exchange in double oral auctions. *The Double Auction Market: Institutions, Theories, and Evidence (Dan Friedman and John Rust, Eds.)*, pages 63–97, 1993.

[30] B. Edelman, M. Ostrovsky, and M. Schwarz. Internet advertising and the generalized second-price auction: Selling billions of dollars worth of keywords. *American Economic Review*, 97(1):242–259, 2007.

[31] M. Fan, J. Stallaert, and A. B. Whinston. The internet and the future of financial markets. *Communications of the ACM*, 43(11):82–88, 2000.

[32] S. Fatima, M. Wooldridge, and N. R. Jennings. Revenue maximising agendas for sequential english auctions. In *Proceedings of the 3rd International Joint Conference on Autonomous Agents and Multiagent Systems*, pages 1432–1433, Washington, DC, USA, 2004. IEEE Computer Society.

[33] S. S. Fatima, M. Wooldridge, and N. R. Jennings. Sequential auctions in uncertain information settings. In *Proceedings of the 9th International Workshop on Agent-Mediated Electronic Commerce*, pages 15–28, 2007.

[34] T. Fraichard and P. Garnier. Fuzzy control to drive car-like vehicles. *Robotics and Autonomous Systems*, 34:1–22, 2001.

[35] M. K. Franklin and M. K. Reiter. The design and implementation of a secure auction service. *IEEE Transactions on Software Engineering*, 22(5):302–312, 1996.

[36] D. Friedman. The double auction market institution: A survey. *The Double Auction Market: Institutions, Theories, and Evidence (Dan Friedman and John Rust, Eds.)*, pages 3–26, 1993.

[37] S. Garfinkel, G. Spafford, and D. Russell. *Web Security, Privacy, and Commerce*. O'Reily, 2001.

[38] E. H. Gerding, A. Rogers, R. K. Dash, and N. R. Jennings. Competing sellers in online markets: reserve prices, shill bidding, and auction fees. In *Proceedings of the 5th International Joint Conference on Autonomous Agents and Multiagent Systems*, pages 1208–1210, New York, NY, USA, 2006. ACM.

[39] E. H. Gerding, A. Rogers, R. K. Dash, and N. R. Jennings. Sellers competing for buyers in online markets: reserve prices, shill bids and auction fees. In *Proceedings of the 20th International Joint Conference on Artificial Intelligence*, pages 1287–1293, 2007.

[40] E. H. Gerding, A. Rogers, D. C. K. Yuen, and N. R. Jennings. Bidding optimally in concurrent second-price auctions of perfectly substitutable goods. In *Proceedings of the 6th International Joint Conference on Autonomous Agents and Multiagent Systems*, pages 267–274, 2007.

[41] S. Gjerstad and J. Dickhaut. Price formation in double auctions. *Games and Economic Behavior*, 22:1–29, 1998.

[42] D. K. Gode and S. Sunder. Allocative efficiency of markets with zero-intelligence traders: Market as a partial substitute for individual rationality. *Journal of Political Economy*, 101(1):119–137, 1993.

[43] D. K. Gode and S. Sunder. Lower bounds for efficiency of surplus extraction in double auctions. *The Double Auction Market: Institutions, Theories, and Evidence (Dan Friedman and John Rust, Eds.)*, pages 199–219, 1993.

[44] M. Goyal, J. Lu, and G. Zhang. A novel fuzzy attitude based bidding strategy for multi-attribute auction. In *Proceedings of the 2006 IEEE/WIC/ACM International Conference on Web Intelligence and Intelligent Agent Technology*, pages 535–539, Washington, DC, USA, 2006. IEEE Computer Society.

[45] F. Gul and E. Stacchetti. The english auction with differentiated commodities. *Journal of Economic Theory*, 92(1):66–95, May 2000.

[46] M. Harkavy, J. D. Tygar, and H. Kikuchi. Electronic auctions with private bids. In *Proceedings of the 3rd Conference on USENIX Workshop on Electronic Commerce*, Berkeley, CA, USA, 1998. USENIX Association.

[47] H. Hattori, T. Ozono, and T. Shintani. Applying a combinatorial auction protocol to a coalition formation among agents in complex problems. In *Proceedings of the 2nd International Joint Conference on Autonomous Agents and Multiagent Systems*, pages 1008–1009, New York, NY, USA, 2003. ACM.

[48] M. He and N. R. Jennings. Southamptontac: An adaptive autonomous trading agent. *ACM Transactions on Internet Technology*, 3(3):218–235, Aug. 2003.

[49] M. He and N. R. Jennings. Designing a successful trading agent:a fuzzy set approach. *IEEE Transactions on Fuzzy Systems*, 12(3):389 – 410, 2004.

[50] M. He, N. R. Jennings, and H. F. Leung. On agent-mediated electronic commerce. *IEEE Transactions on Knowledge and Data Engineering*, 15(4):985–1003, Jul./Aug. 2003.

[51] M. He, N. R. Jennings, and A. Prügel-Bennett. A heuristic bidding strategy for buying multiple goods in multiple english auctions. *ACM Transaction on Internet Technology*, 6(4):465–496, 2006.

[52] M. He and H. F. Leung. An agent bidding strategy based on fuzzy logic in a continuous double auction. In *Proceedings of the 2001 IEEE International Conference on Systems, Man, and Cybernetics*, volume 1, pages 583–588, 2001.

[53] M. He, H. F. Leung, and N. R. Jennings. A fuzzy-logic based bidding strategy for autonomous agents in continuous double auctions. *IEEE Transactions on Knowledge and Data Engineering*, 15(6), Nov./Dec. 2003.

[54] P. Huang and K. Sycara. Computational model for online agent negotiation. In *Proceedings of the 35th Annual Hawaii International Conference on System Sciences*, Washington, DC, USA, 2002. IEEE Computer Society.

[55] B. Hudson and T. Sandholm. Effectiveness of query types and policies for preference elicitation in combinatorial auctions. In *Proceedings of the 3rd International Joint Conference on Autonomous Agents and Multiagent Systems*, pages 386–393, Washington, DC, USA, 2004. IEEE Computer Society.

[56] L. Hunsberger and B. J. Grosz. A combinatorial auction for collaborative planning. In *Proceedings of the 4th International Conference on Multiagent Systems*, pages 151–158, Washington, DC, USA, 2000. IEEE Computer Society.

[57] T. Ito, M. Yokoo, and S. Matsubara. A combinatorial auction protocol among versatile experts and amateurs. In *Proceedings of the 3rd International Joint Conference on Autonomous Agents and Multiagent Systems*, pages 378–385, Washington, DC, USA, 2004. IEEE Computer Society.

[58] N. R. Jennings. An agent-based approach for building complex software systems. *Communications of The ACM*, 44(4):35–41, 2001.

[59] D. Kehagias, P. Toulis, and P. A. Mitkas. A long-term profit seeking strategy for continuous double auctions in a trading agent competition. In G. Antoniou, G. Potamias, C. Spyropoulos, and D. Plexousakis, editors, *Proceedings of the 4th Helenic Conference on Artificial Intelligence*, volume 3955 of *Lecture Notes in Computer Science*, pages 116–126. Springer, 2006.

[60] M. Kumar and S. I. Feldman. Internet auctions. In *Proceedings of the 3rd Conference on USENIX Workshop on Electronic Commerce*, pages 49–60, Berkeley, CA, USA, 1998. USENIX Association.

[61] K. M. Lam and H. F. Leung. An adaptive strategy for trust/honesty model in multi-agent semi-competitive environments. In *Proceedings of the 16th IEEE International Conference on Tools with Artificial Intelligence*, pages 416–423, 2004.

[62] H. B. Leonard. Elicitation of honest preferences for the assignment of individuals to positions. *Journal of Political Economy*, 91(3):461–479, 1983.

[63] L. Li and S. F. Smith. Speculation agents for dynamic multi-period continuous double auctions in b2b exchanges. In *Proceedings of the Proceedings of the 37th Annual Hawaii International Conference on System Sciences*, pages 1–9, Washington, DC, USA, 2004. IEEE Computer Society.

[64] Y. Liu, R. Goodwin, and S. Koenig. Risk-averse auction agents. In *Proceedings of the 2nd International Joint Conference on Autonomous Agents and Multiagent Systems*, pages 353–360, New York, NY, USA, 2003. ACM.

[65] D. Lucking-Reiley. Using field experiments to test equivalence between auction formats: Magic on the internet. *The American Economic Review*, pages 1063–1080, 1999.

[66] X. Luo and N. R. Jennings. A spectrum of compromise aggregation operators for multi-attribute decision making. *Artificial Intelligence Journal*, 171(2-3):161–184, 2007.

[67] H. Ma and H. F. Leung. An adaptive attitude bidding strategy for agents in continuous double auctions. In *Proceedings of the 2005 IEEE International Conference on E-Technology, E-Commerce and E-Service*, pages 38–43, Washington, DC, USA, Mar 2005. IEEE Computer Society.

[68] H. Ma and H. F. Leung. Adaptive soft bid determination in bidding strategies for continuous double auctions. In *Proceedings of the 17th IEEE International Conference on Tools with Artificial Intelligence*, Hong Kong, China, Nov. 2005.

[69] H. Ma and H. F. Leung. The effect of price acceptability to agents in continuous double auctions. In *Technical Report of Dept. of CSE, Chinese University of Hong Kong*, 2005.

[70] H. Ma and H. F. Leung. Enhancing bidding strategies in cdas by adaptive judgement of price acceptability. In *Proceedings of the 8th Pacific Rim International Workshop on Multiagents*, Kuala Lumpur, Malaysia, Sep. 2005.

[71] H. Ma and H. F. Leung. Effect of time strategies on the profit of agents using adaptive bid softness determination in continuous double auctions with a fixed deadline. In *Proceedings of 2006 IEEE Joint Conference on E-Commerce Technology and Enterprise Computing, E-Commerce and E-Services*, pages 16–23, Washington, DC, USA, June 2006. IEEE Computer Society.

[72] H. Ma and H. F. Leung. Adaptive agents for sequential english auctions with a fixed deadline. In *Proceedings of 2007 IEEE Joint Conference on E-Commerce Technology and Enterprise Computing, E-Commerce and E-Services*, pages 29–38, Tokyo, Japan, July 2007.

[73] H. Ma and H. F. Leung. An adaptive attitude bidding strategy for agents in continuous double auctions. *Electronic Commerce Research and Applications*, 6(4):383–398, 2007.

[74] R. P. McAfee and J. McMillan. Auctions and bidding. *Journal of Economic Literature*, 25(2):699–738, Jun. 1987.

[75] P. McDermott. Building trust into online business. *Network Security*, 10:10–12, 2000.

[76] P. Milgrom. Auction theory. *Advances in Economic Theory: 5th World Congress (T. Bewley Eds.)*, pages 1–32, 1985.

[77] P. Milgrom. Auctions and bidding: A primer. *Journal of Economic Perspectives*, 3(3):3–22, 1989.

[78] P. R. Milgrom and R. J. Weber. A theory of auctions and competitive bidding. *Econometrica*, 50(5):1089–1122, 1982.

[79] M. Mitchell. *An Introduction to Genetic Algorithms*. MIT Press, 1996.

[80] L. Mui, A. Halberstadt, and M. Mohtashemi. Motions of reputation in multi-agent systems: A review. In *Proceedings of the 1st International Joint Conference of Autonomous Agents and Multiagent Systems*, pages 280–287, July 2002.

[81] S. Murugesan. Negotiation by software agents in electronic marketplace. In *Proceedings of TENCON*, pages 286–290, 2000.

[82] M. Naor, B. Pinkas, and R. Sumner. Privacy preserving auctions and mechanism design. In *EC '99: Proceedings of the 1st ACM Conference on Electronic Commerce*, pages 129–139, New York, NY, USA, 1999. ACM.

[83] H. S. Nwana. Software agents: An overview. *Knowledge Engineering Review*, 11(3):1–40, Sep. 1996.

[84] A. Ockenfels and A. E. Roth. The timing of bids in internet auctions: Market design, bidder behavior, and artificial agents. *AI Magazine*, pages 79–88, 2002.

[85] A. Ockenfels and A. E. Roth. Late and multiple bidding in second-price internet auctions: Theory and evidence concerning different rules for ending an auction. *Games and Economic Behavior*, 55:297–320, 2006.

[86] S. Park, E. H. Durfee, and W. P. Birmingham. An adaptive agent bidding strategy based on stochastic modeling. In *Proceedings of the 3rd annual Conference on Autonomous Agents*, pages 147–153, New York, NY, USA, 1999. ACM.

[87] J. M. Perloff. *Microeconomics*. Addison Wesley, 1998.

[88] C. R. Plott. Industrial organization theory and experimental economics. *Journal of Economic Literature*, 20(4):1485–1527, December 1982.

[89] C. Preist. Economic agents for automated trading. Technical Report HPL-98-77, Bristol, UK, April 1998.

[90] C. Preist. Commodity trading using an agent-based iterated double auction. In *Proceedings of the 3rd annual Conference on Autonomous Agents*, pages 131–138, New York, NY, USA, 1999. ACM.

[91] C. Preist, A. Byde, and C. Bartolini. Economic dynamics of agents in multiple auctions. In *Proceedings of the 5th International Conference on Autonomous Agents*, pages 545–551, New York, NY, USA, 2001. ACM.

[92] C. Preist and M. van Tol. Adaptive agents in a persistent shout double auction. In *Proceedings of the 1st International Conference on Information and Computation Economies*, pages 11–18, New York, NY, USA, 1998. ACM.

[93] A. Rogers, E. David, J. Schiff, and N. R. Jennings. The effects of proxy bidding and minimum bid increments within ebay auctions. *ACM Transactions on the Web*, 1(2), 2007.

[94] A. E. Roth and A. Ockenfels. Last-minute bidding and the rules of ending second-price auctions: Evidence from ebay and amazon auctions on the internet. *American Economic Review*, 92(4):1093–1103, 2002.

[95] J. Rykowski and W. Cellary. Virtual web services: application of software agents to personalization of web services. In *Proceedings of the 6th International Conference on Electronic Commerce*, pages 409–418, New York, NY, USA, 2004. ACM.

[96] A. Sadrieh. *The Alternating Double Auction Market: A Game Theoretic and Experimental Investigation.* Springer, 1998.

[97] T. Sandholm. *Distributed Rational Decision Making In G. Weiss (ed). Multiagent Systems.* MIT PRESS, Cambridge, MA, 1999.

[98] M. Schillo, P. Funk, and M. Rovatsos. Using trust for detecting deceitful agents in artificial societies. *Applied Artificial Intelligence*, 14(8):825–848, 2000.

[99] E. Schwartz. At on-line auctions, good and raw deals. *New York Times, Circuit Section*, 5 March (1998), 1998.

[100] K. Sim. A market-driven model for designing negotiation agents. *Computational Intelligence*, 18(4):618–637, 2002.

[101] V. Smith. An experimental study of competitive market behavior. *Journal of Political Economy*, 70(2):111–137, 1962.

[102] V. Smith and A. Williams. *An Experimental Study of Alternative Rules for Competitive Market Exchange in Auctions, Bidding and Contracting: Uses and Theory*. New York University Press, 1983.

[103] J. Song and J. Baker. An integrated model exploring sellers' strategies in ebay auctions. *Electronic Commerce Research*, 7(2):165–187, 2007.

[104] S. Subramanian. Design and verification of a secure electronic auction protocol. In *Proceedings of the The 17th IEEE Symposium on Reliable Distributed Systems*, Washington, DC, USA, 1998. IEEE Computer Society.

[105] M. Sugeno. An introductory survey of fuzzy control. *Information Sciences*, 36:59–83, 1985.

[106] P. J. 't Hoen and J. A. L. Poutre. Repeated auctions with complementarities. *Agent-Mediated Electronic Commerce. Designing Trading Agents and Mechanisms*, pages 16–29, 2006.

[107] G. Tesauro and J. L. Bredin. Strategic sequential bidding in auctions using dynamic programming. In *Proceedings of the 1st International Joint Conference on Autonomous Agents and Multiagent Systems*, pages 591–598, New York, NY, USA, 2002. ACM.

[108] G. Tesauro and R. Das. High-performance bidding agents for the continuous double auction. In *Proceedings of the 3rd ACM Conference on Electronic Commerce*, pages 206–209, New York, NY, USA, 2001. ACM.

[109] P. Toulis, D. Kehagias, and P. A. Mitkas. Mertacor: a successful autonomous trading agent. In *Proceedings of the 5th International Joint Conference on Autonomous Agents and Multiagent Systems*, pages 1191–1198, New York, NY, USA, 2006. ACM.

[110] Y. A. Tung, R. D. Gopal, and A. B. Whinston. Multiple online auctions. *IEEE Computer*, 36(2):100–102, Feb 2003.

[111] E. Turban, J. Lee, D. King, and H. M. C. eds. *Electronic Commerce: A Managerial Perspective*. Prentice Hall, 1999.

[112] A. Vakali, L. Angelis, and D. Pournara. Internet based auctions: A survey on models and applications. *ACM SIGecom Exchanges*, 2(2):6–15, 2001.

[113] H. R. Varian. Economic mechanism design for computerized agents. In *Proceedings of the 1st Conference on USENIX Workshop on Electronic Commerce*, Berkeley, CA, USA, 1995. USENIX Association.

[114] W. Vickrey. Counterspeculation, auctions, and competitive sealed tenders. *Journal of Finance*, 16(1).

[115] P. Vytelingum, D. Cliff, and N. R. Jenning. Evolutionary stability of behavioural types in the continuous double auction. In *Proceedings of 8th International Workshop on Agent-Mediated Electronic Commerce*, Hakodate, Japan, 2006.

[116] P. Vytelingum, R. K. Dash, E. David, and N. R. Jenning. A risk-based bidding strategy for continuous double auctions. In *Proceedings of 16th European Conference on Artificial Intelligence*, pages 79–83, 2004.

[117] P. Vytelingum, R. K. Dash, M. He, and N. R. Jenning. A framework for designing strategies for trading agents. In *Proceedings of IJCAI Workshop on Trading Agent Design and Analysis*, Edinburgh, Scotland, 2005.

[118] W. E. Walsh, M. P. Wellman, and F. Ygge. Combinatorial auctions for supply chain formation. In *Proceedings of the 2nd ACM Conference on Electronic Commerce*, pages 260–269, New York, NY, USA, 2000. ACM.

[119] H. A. Wan, A. Hunter, and P. Dunne. Autonomous agent models of stock markets. *Artificial Intelligence Review*, 17(2):87–128, 2002.

[120] C. Wang and H. F. Leung. Mobile agents for secure electronic commerce transactions with privacy protection of the customers. In *Proceedings of the 2005 IEEE International Conference on E-Technology, E-Commerce and E-Service*, pages 530–535, Washington, DC, USA, 2005. IEEE Computer Society.

[121] W. Wang, Z. Hidvégi, and A. B. Whinston. Economic mechanism design for securing online auctions. In *Proceedings of the 21st International Conference on Information Systems*, pages 676–680, Atlanta, GA, USA, 2000. Association for Information Systems.

[122] Y. Watanabe and H. Imai. Reducing the round complexity of a sealed-bid auction protocol with an off-line ttp. In *Proceedings of the 7th ACM Conference on Computer and Communications Security*, pages 80–86, New York, NY, USA, 2000. ACM.

[123] M. P. Wellman, P. R. Jordan, C. Kiekintveld, J. Miller, and D. M. Reeves. Empirical game-theoretic analysis of the tac market games. In *Proceedings of AAMAS-06 Workshop on Game-Theoretic and Decision-Theoretic Agents*, 2006.

[124] M. P. Wellman, P. R. Wurman, K. O'Malley, R. Bangera, S. de Lin, D. Reeves, and W. E. Walsh. Designing the market game for a trading agent competition. *IEEE Internet Computing*, 5(2):43–51, 2001.

[125] W. Wen and F. Mizoguchi. An authorization-based trust model for multiagent systems. *Applied Artificial Intelligence*, 14(9):909–925, 2000.

[126] H. C. Wong and K. Sycara. Adding security and trust to multiagent systems. *Applied Artificial Intelligence*, 14(9):927–941, 2000.

[127] M. Wooldridge and N. R. Jennings. Intelligent agents: Theory and practice. *The Knowledge Engeering Review*, 10(2):115–152, 1995.

[128] P. R. Wurman. Dynamic pricing in the virtual marketplace. *IEEE Internet Computing*, pages 36–42, March/April 2001.

[129] P. R. Wurman and M. P. Wellman. Akba: A progressive, anonymous-price combinatorial auction. In *Proceedings of the ACM Conference on Electronic Commerce*, pages 21–29, Minneapolis, Minnesota, Oct. 2000.

[130] P. R. Wurman, M. P. Wellman, and W. E. Walsh. The michigan internet auctionbot: a configurable auction server for human and software agents. In *Proceedings of the 2nd International Conference on Autonomous Agents*, pages 301–308, New York, NY, USA, 1998. ACM.

[131] J. Yao and J. Yao. Fuzzy decision making for medical diagnosis based on fuzzy number and compositional rule of inference. *Fuzzy Sets and systems*, 120:351–366, 2001.

[132] D. Yuen, A. Byde, and N. R. Jennings. Heuristic bidding strategies for multiple heterogeneous auctions. In *Proceedings of the 17th European Conference on Artificial Intelligence*, pages 300–304, 2006.

[133] L. Zadeh. Fuzzy sets. *Information and Control*, 12:338–353, 1965.

[134] H. J. Zimmermann. *Fuzzy Set Theory and Its Applications*. Kluwer Academic Publishers, 1996.

Index

BIRKHÄUSER

WHITESTEIN SERIES IN SOFTWARE
AGENT TECHNOLOGIES AND AUTONOMIC

CASCOM: Intelligent Service Coordination in the Semantic Web

Schumacher, M., Av. du Grammont, Lausanne, Switzerland / **Helin, H.**, TeliaSonera, Finland / **Schuldt, H.**, Universität Basel, Switzerland (eds)

2008. Approx. 250 pp. Softcover
ISBN 978-3-7643-8574-3

This book presents the design, implementation and validation of a value-added supportive infrastructure for Semantic Web based business application services across mobile and fixed networks, applied to an emergency healthcare application. This infrastructure has been realized by the CASCOM European research project. For end users, the CASCOM framework provides seamless access to semantic Web services anytime, anywhere, by using any mobile computing device. For service providers, CASCOM offers an innovative development platform for intelligent and mobile business application services in the Semantic Web.

From the contents:
Innovative research results and techniques for context-aware, agent-based business application service coordination and secure provision in open P2P service environments.- Design and implementation of context-aware agents using these techniques, and basic co-ordination infrastructure services.- Service coordination architecture and specifications, and guidelines for using and developing various context-aware business application services in nomadic computing environments.- A prototypically implemented service coordination demonstrator for an emergency healthcare use case scenario.

www.birkhauser.ch

Whitestein Series in Software Agent Technologies and Autonomic Computing

Edited by

Marius Walliser, Stefan Brantschen, Monique Calisti and Marc Herbstritt

This series reports new developments in agent-based software technologies and agent-oriented software engineering methodologies, with particular emphasis on applications in the area of autonomic computing and communications.

The spectrum of the series includes research monographs, high quality notes resulting from research and industrial projects, outstanding Ph.D. theses, and the proceedings of carefully selected conferences. The series is targeted at promoting advanced research and facilitating know-how transfer to industrial use.

■ **Pěchouček, M.**, Czech Technical University, Prague, Czech Republic / **Thompson, S.G.**, BT. Labs, Suffolk, U.K. / **Voos, H.**, University of Applied Sciences, Ravensburg-Weingarten, Germany (eds.)

Defense Industry Applications of Autonomous Agents and Multi-Agent Systems

Defense and security related applications are increasingly being tackled using technologies developed in the field of Intelligent Agent research. This book is a collection of recent refereed papers drawn from workshops and other colloquia held in various venues around the world in the last two years. The contributions in this book describe work in the development of command and control systems, military communications systems, information systems, surveillance systems, autonomous vehicles, simulators and Human Computer Interactions. The broad nature of the application domain is matched by the diversity of techniques used in the papers that are included in the collection that provides, for the first time, an overview of the most significant work being performed by the leading workers in this area. It provides a single reference point for the state of the art in the field and will be of interest to Computer Science professionals working in the defense sector, and academics investigating the technology of Intelligent Agents that are curious to see how the technology is applied in practice.

2007. 180 pages. Softcover.
ISBN 978-3-7643-8570-5

■ **Calisti, M.**, Whitestein Technologies AG, Zürich, Switzerland / **van der Meer, S.**, Waterford Institute of Technology, Ireland / **Strassner, J.**, Motorola, Inc., Schaumburg, IL, USA (eds.)

Advanced Autonomic Networking and Communication

This book presents a comprehensive reference of state-of-the-art efforts and early results in the area of autonomic networking and communication.

The essence of autonomic networking, and thus autonomic communication, is to enable self-governing of services and resources within the constraints of business rules. In order to support self-governance, appropriate self-* functionality will be deployed in the network on an application-specific basis. The continuing increase in complexity of upcoming networking convergence scenarios mandates a new approach to network management.

The book consists of three three parts consisting of papers from industrial and academic perspectives. The first part focuses on architec- tures and modeling strategies. Part two is dedicated to middleware and service infrastructure as facilitators of autonomic communications. The last part addresses autonomic networks, specifically how networks can be equipped with autonomic functionality and thus migrate to autonomic networks.

2007. 200 pages. Softcover.
ISBN 978-3-7643-8568-2

■ **Annicchiarico, R.**, Fondazione Santa Lucia IRCCS, Rome, Italy / **Cortés, U.**, Universidad Malaga, Spain / **Urdiales, C.**, Universidad Polytècnica de Catalunya, Barcelona, Spain (eds.)

Agent Technology and e-Health

2007. 156 pages. Softcover.
ISBN 978-3-7643-8546-0

■ **Moreno, A.** University of Tarragona, Spain / **Pavón, J.**, University of Madrid, Spain (eds.)

Issues in Multi-Agent Systems The AgentCities.ES Experience

2007. 240 pages. Softcover.
ISBN 978-3-7643-8542-2

■ **Pautasso, C.**, IBM Zürich, Switzerland / **Bussler, C.**, Cisco Systems Inc., San Jose, USA (eds.)

Emerging Web Services Technology

2007. 182 pages. Softcover.
ISBN 978-3-7643-8447-0

BIRKHÄUSER